A JOURNEY
INTO AUDITING CULTURE

A Story and a Practical Guide

Susan Jex, FRSA

Eddie J. Best, FCA

Published by the Internal Audit Foundation
1035 Greenwood Blvd., Suite 401
Lake Mary, Florida 32746, USA

Limit of Liability: The Internal Audit Foundation publishes this document for informational and educational purposes and is not a substitute for legal or accounting advice. The Foundation does not provide such advice and makes no warranty as to any legal or accounting results through its publication of this document. When legal or accounting issues arise, professional assistance should be sought and retained.

The IIA's International Professional Practices Framework (IPPF) comprises the full range of existing and developing practice guidance for the profession. The IPPF provides guidance to internal auditors globally and paves the way to world-class internal auditing.

The IIA and the Foundation work in partnership with researchers from around the globe who conduct valuable studies on critical issues affecting today's business world. Much of the content presented in their final reports is a result of Foundation-funded research and prepared as a service to the Foundation and the internal audit profession. Expressed opinions, interpretations, or points of view represent a consensus of the researchers and do not necessarily reflect or represent the official position or policies of The IIA or the Foundation.

ISBN-13: 978-1-63454-056-8

23 22 21 20 19   1 2 3 4 5 6

Printed in Canada

Contents

Foreword

The world of internal auditing is changing fast, and organisations are looking to us for more sophisticated and strategic insights to the risks they face. We have a seat at the table. It was hard fought and we need to make it count, both for our profession and for our organisations and their success.

However, it is increasingly the case that subjects such as people risk and culture risk are the major organisational challenges. These are areas where internal auditors have not historically had strong capabilities or solid frameworks for assessing and auditing them. They are difficult issues, often seen as intangible and unmanageable, too complex to audit or pin down. But good business leaders do lead, own, and manage them. By utilising frameworks set out in this book, we can walk the journey with those leaders and ensure that cultures are properly embedded in a way that can really help organisations achieve their business goals.

We continue to learn as a profession, and we can continue to add in new tools to this framework. Sentiment analysis is becoming a great tool for us to assess communication and engagement, as well as data analytics and artificial intelligence. It is incumbent on all of us to add to the internal audit toolbox and be better strategic partners to our organisations—even when the topic seems complex or seemingly intangible.

— **Jason Davies**
Chief Audit and Risk Officer,
Tesco plc

About the Authors

Susan Jex, FRSA, is the culture lead within the Business Risk Services team at Grant Thornton and has designed the methodology for culture audit across the firm. She has undertaken culture audits across a number of firms and sectors, including at a major global retailer, and has undertaken HR value-added audits across many organisations, in both cases liaising at board level linking strategy and the achievement of business goals with culture.

She previously worked at HSBC as group head of diversity and group head of employee relations, amongst other roles. As head of customer service and culture, she developed an integrated and holistic approach to culture and client service, implementing business wide and driving through to delivery. The culture programme saw the bank move from bottom to top of the industry customer satisfaction index in just two years.

She also helped to develop the brand and marketing strategy of HSBC globally, leading to the launch of "The World's Local Bank." She is BA (Hons), a fellow of the Chartered Institute of Certified Accountants, and a Fellow of the Royal Society of Arts.

Eddie J. Best, FCA, is the global co-leader of the Business Risk Services team at Grant Thornton. He specialises in providing risk-based internal audit and transformation assurance services to global organisations, a significant aspect of which relates to protecting and transforming people and culture-based assets and value.

He has extensive experience supporting our international listed clients with the development and implementation of global risk management and internal audit, supporting a number of major clients as they embark on significant people and culture change programmes in order to pursue their strategic and regulatory objectives.

Eddie works closely with colleagues around the world to provide cohesive expert support to clients. He is BA (Hons), a Fellow of the Institute of Chartered Accountants in England & Wales, and an affiliate of The IIA.

Introduction

The topic of auditing culture is relatively new and is a challenging one for internal audit, as the risks and controls are more difficult to identify, assess, and audit. There are a number of emerging approaches to this type of audit, and this book provides both suggested approaches and a framework of areas to consider when examining the topic.

We meet Alex, the head of Internal Audit for Shapers Inc., a global organisation working across a number of sectors. Alex is asked by the CEO to audit culture and, like many of us, is unsure of where to start. Each chapter is structured to cover both Alex's challenge and his story—his journey of exploration into this fascinating new area for audit. The research and technical tools behind the areas he is discovering then follow, then key success factors, and, finally, important questions you should ask in your audit of culture in your own organisation. The story is shown in grey type and the technical elements, success factors, and questions are in black type.

There is much academic research and organisational experience in the area of culture change. As auditors, we look to learn from that experience but also to add our own expertise in risk and controls, in design and operational effectiveness, and so arrive at a framework and approach that provides both actionable findings, risk ratings, and reports that add real value to the organisations we are supporting. Culture itself is dynamic and changes over time, and we can see this as we explore how to audit it. There are many factors influencing—and therefore altering—the culture of an organisation.

Our thanks go to those who assisted us in talking through concepts, encouraging us, developing thoughts, and making introductions, in particular Warren Stippich, Sandy Kumar, Howard Miller, Graham Jackson, and Paul Cook.

A valued colleague from Switzerland once told us that any book introduction needs a quote. So, with thanks to Patrick, the Financial Conduct Authority in the UK tells us:

"A good culture means more than ensuring that good people don't do bad things—it is about enabling good people to do even better things. Only an ethical culture based on principles will enable people to make good decisions when they have no precedent or rule to turn to."

The book is also designed to be an enjoyable read. We hope you find it so.

A JOURNEY

INTO AUDITING CULTURE

A Story and a Practical Guide

The Challenge

Alex, the head of Internal Audit, closed the door to the board meeting and wondered just what on earth he had agreed to do. Only moments earlier he had been in the meeting and all was going well, until Sam announced that she had been talking to the audit committee chair and they both agreed an audit of their corporate culture was needed. At that point, everyone looked at Sam as though she was a bit crazy. Even Alex wondered how such a wispy issue as culture could even be defined, let alone audited. However, Alex had great respect for Sam. She was the CEO of Shapers Inc., a large organisation that had operations across the globe with different brands in various sectors.

In the time that Sam had been in her post, she had started to make a number of changes to drive the business forward. The previous CEO had been competent but hadn't set the company alight with new ideas or fresh thinking. In fact, some parts of the organisation were outdated in their operation and offering. It was because of her new way of doing things and making change that Alex found himself in the meeting agreeing that culture was a major area of focus for all successful companies, and that he would find a way to audit it.

Sam had smiled at him and asked for a timeline. She had suggested a month, but Alex knew that he would need longer as there was a lot to cover. In the end, they agreed on two months. That tied in nicely with the next board meeting at which Alex would present his findings. His instinct told Alex to make sure he did a proper job rather than a rushed one. He knew how important the subject of culture was. After all, it was discussed often enough, both at other internal audit forums and with senior executives. But he felt that it was perhaps only at a high level and no one really took a structured deep dive into the issue. He was due to report back with his outline plan at the Monday morning meeting in just 10 working days. A challenge is good for self-development, he thought.

His stomach rumbled and he found himself a table at the office canteen. No one joined him, which was a blessing, as he ate and thought about what he understood culture to mean. Alex was hungry as breakfast had been almost nonexistent. He had time only for a cup of black coffee and some yoghurt. Whilst thinking about his breakfast, a business phrase landed in his subconscious. Don't chase it, he thought. It is sure to come back at some point.

The canteen began filling up for the lunch hour rush. Everyone seemed very chatty and positive and, whilst he didn't eavesdrop, Alex heard snippets of conversation from time to time. He found out that one of the units was seriously fed up as they were going to have a whole IT system replaced but hadn't been involved in any of the decision making. At that moment, the chief technology officer (CTO) appeared and the gossip came to a collective halt.

Alex smiled to himself. A company drama that maybe wasn't so important after all. It then clicked. He remembered the expression, or at least some of it. Two words came to mind: breakfast and strategy. He couldn't quite get the whole expression, but he could of course "Google it" when he got back to work.

Back at his desk, with a full stomach and the drive to get on and find out more about the nebulous topic of culture, Alex fired up his laptop, checked a few emails for anything urgent, and then began to tap away and gather information that would help him on his exploration of organisational culture.

He soon found the phrase that had troubled him earlier. It was the classic phrase originally from Peter Drucker and made famous by Mark Fields, president at Ford, "Culture eats strategy for breakfast." Alex filed it away for future reference, but he had a sneaking suspicion that he would end up challenging the phrase rather than blindly accepting it. After all, it was his job to ask questions and find answers.

He loved his job and knew he and his team made a huge difference to the organisation, but he knew that his role was changing whether he liked it or not. For him to stay relevant and continue to make a contribution to the success of the company, he would have to move with the times. More than that, he would have to help take the company to the next level. It was this feeling that had led him to embrace the challenge at the earlier meeting.

Part of his reasoning was also steeped in fact. He was an avid reader of numerous business magazines and he also listened to business podcasts. He liked to have a good understanding as to what was happening in the business world around him. Two things were clear to him. Firstly, some of the work undertaken by internal auditors was now being carried out via technology. Artificial intelligence was coming on in leaps and bounds. Even with the current technology, crunching numbers and presenting them was becoming even faster. Secondly, there was a direct correlation between the success of an organisation and its focus on culture and people. He didn't know enough about the people and culture connection as yet, but he knew there was something in it.

Yes, Alex felt the future of internal audit was going to be exciting and different. He knew that this was a new opportunity, one that went beyond traditional process and control, more connected to people across the organisation, and a critical topic affecting every part of the company. Information around culture had started to become invaluable for senior leadership. From the meeting earlier in the day, some of the leadership comments had surprised him. Surely they knew what "culture" was and how it played a part. Perhaps they would all be learning together!

Alex was deep in concentration when Bill, the chief operating officer (COO), approached him. "I see something has grabbed your attention," Bill said.

"Yes, it sure has. I am doing some research on organisational culture to enable me to present ideas on how to audit it for the next board meeting," Alex replied.

A big smile came over Bill's face. "Good luck with that, my friend. You will have more of a chance in trying to catch a moonbeam," he said.

With that, Bill turned and left Alex to carry on with his work. Alex would find a way to prove him wrong. There must be a way to audit culture, and he was determined to find it.

His day at the office finished, he packed up and headed home. Once home, he parked all of his thoughts of the day and set off on his daily five-mile run. Running was a big part of Alex's life. He liked to keep fit and the run really helped him unwind.

Where was he running to on his journey into culture and what would he find along the way, he wondered, as he settled down into a steady pace. His exploration had begun.

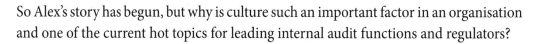

So Alex's story has begun, but why is culture such an important factor in an organisation and one of the current hot topics for leading internal audit functions and regulators?

Structured risk assessments across business lines, key risk areas, and functions really help in understanding risk, the audit universe, and in planning across an audit cycle. However, the historic focus on hard data and specific processes has potentially led to things being missed. If we look at the financial services sector over the last 10 years, a focus on specific conduct processes meant behavioural risks were not typically included in the audit universe, the risk management framework, or the compliance plan. The regulatory focus on "conduct" post 2007 and the identification of tangible conduct measures was an important step; however, it was not enough, and the subsequent focus on risk culture broadened the scope of audits in this area considerably. Internal audit is beginning to go further than this and really understand the enterprise-level behavioural risks within a business and be able to form an opinion on them, adding value and understanding to both first and second lines. Internal audit really can audit organisational culture and this book explores how. It looks at how many organisations are tackling this issue, what the trends are, and what the early results and developing methodologies are showing.

Like many a construction project, building a "corporate culture" needs building blocks. But what do we mean by "culture"? In other walks of life, culture is a concept all of us are familiar with. Yet, the business community has been playing catch-up in defining corporate culture and the elements that create it.

One definition of corporate culture is "the combination of values, attitudes, and behaviours that a company exhibits in its operations and relations with those affected by its conduct, e.g., employees, customers, suppliers, and wider society." Wijnand Nuijts of the Department of Governance, Culture and Organisation Behaviour at the Dutch National Bank drew two conclusions:

"That culture is not a monolithic, but a multifaceted construct that includes numerous components. These components are not tied together through hierarchy, nor through a linear causal relationship. Rather, they constantly mutually influence each other in a continuous cyclical process."

And,

"That culture is not static and does not exist in isolation. In fact, culture is (the product of) an adaptive response to environmental influences (at a certain point in time) and develops in order to address the challenges that are created by the internal and external environment. This evolutionary aspect of culture has implications for the manner in which supervisors can, or perhaps even should, supervise culture."

Others will put it differently. What's undeniable though is that around the world, the issue of corporate culture is receiving increased attention as a foundation of good governance and indeed a driver of performance. As a result, culture has arguably never been as high up the business agenda as it is today. If any more evidence were needed of the importance of culture within governance, take a look at any recent press coverage of organisational scandals and a significant number will talk about culture and the role it played.

The survey results contained in Grant Thornton's 2017 report *Beyond Compliance – The building blocks of strong corporate culture* showed that 50% of businesses worldwide have culture as a standing item on their board agenda, while 71% have established internal controls that address culture and employee behaviour. Practices such as benchmarking against peers and exploring customer relationships are also prevalent. The more developed organisations are expanding their internal auditors' remit to test how embedded culture is at all levels of their company.

Boards are heading in the right direction when it comes to culture, but more can be done. After all, regulators (and auditors) cannot develop or embed corporate culture. Culture can only be authentic—and sustainable—if it comes from the leadership of the organisation and is important enough to feature as a key part of its strategy.

We will learn more across all of these topics, and also follow Alex as he continues on his journey.

Key Success Factors

- Active sponsorship and engagement from the board
- Understanding and a desire to embed a positive culture from senior executives

Important Questions

- Does your organisation have a clear purpose and vision?
- Does your board place importance on culture and actively discuss it alongside, or as part of, the strategy?

Exploring from the Desk – Strategy

Following his run and a peaceful night of sleep, Alex awoke refreshed. He had come to the conclusion that today he would need to start with learning about what would take him forward on his latest task of understanding culture. It was clear to him that he would need to understand the issue of "organisational culture" before he could consider coming up with a way to audit it.

He decided to start with what was familiar and dug out the latest audit reports. Alex knew that the culture audit would definitely not be traditional in either shape or form, and would be different to what had gone before, but he also expected that past findings could form part of his emerging view.

Amongst his pile of reports, he found old favourites, which included employee engagement surveys, absenteeism reports, HR audits, profit and loss accounts, financial reports of sales across divisions, sales across countries, and a whole host of supporting documentation that added depth to the papers. He found that despite having a volume of paper on his desk and on his bookshelves, there was still something missing. He didn't know quite what it was, which was starting to frustrate him. After all, a 10-day deadline for the initial plan was a tight timescale to work to.

He didn't panic. He still had time. He decided to take a break and grab a smoothie from the refreshments area. Kamala was also there taking a well-deserved break and, as she was great at reading moods and body language of people, she couldn't help noticing that Alex was anxious about something.

"Why so serious?" she asked him.

Alex then told her about what had happened in the exec meeting and how he had been asked to undertake an audit of culture.

"That sounds rather exciting and a great thing for the company to be doing," she said. "Did you know that the success of many companies these days centres on the culture they have? I am happy to help you on your quest if that helps. Why don't you take a look at our Mission Statement as a starting point?" she suggested.

Before Alex could thank her, she was gone as her phone had bleeped at her, reminding her of the need to be elsewhere. Alex knew which department she worked in and so he would definitely be taking up her offer of help. Kamala was in communications and really skilled at her craft.

Now what was that about the Mission Statement? That must be somewhere. He knew where to find the Vision Statement. It was on the company intranet and stared back at him every time he logged on. He looked at it every day but had ceased to take any notice of what it was really saying. He would have to look at it more closely when he got back to his desk.

Kamala had told Alex that "a Vision Statement focuses on tomorrow and what the organisation wants to become, whereas a Mission Statement focuses on today and what the organisation does. While a company commonly uses mission and vision statements interchangeably, it needs both. One doesn't work without the other, because having purpose and meaning are critical for any business."

He was delighted when he found the Mission Statement, which was proudly pinned to the notice board in the canteen area. It crossed his mind as to whether that was the best position for it and whether it should be displayed elsewhere for all to see.

Pleased that he had located the documents, he felt that he was making progress. But he was still wrestling with the "culture eats strategy for breakfast" quote that he had discovered the day before.

If the strategy is eaten by whatever culture is, then what happens to the organisation? Surely the strategy is key to the overall direction of the company. He also mused that once culture had eaten breakfast, what would it do for lunch and dinner? In all seriousness though, could culture and strategy not live in harmony together? Surely they were both needed for the business to be successful. Alex had been looking at different definitions of culture in business and felt that he had some basics to get him further on with this exploration, but there was so much to it.

Feeling overwhelmed, he looked out his window and let his thoughts roam. Where would he find the strategy of the company? Where was it? Was it written down? Who had access to it?

Whilst Alex was the head of Internal Audit, he wanted to make sure that he was not making any assumptions and felt that starting at the beginning with no preconceived ideas would serve him best. He had to understand what the strategy meant in practice. How was it being carried forward by the leaders and staff working within the various branches and divisions around the globe?

There was only so much that he would achieve by sitting at his desk. Alex needed a plan. He realised that a single perspective from his office in London wouldn't be enough for his task. He called his assistant, Isobella, and rattled off a list of offices he wanted to visit. He gave her the dates she could use and then left her to make the travel plans and other logistics to help make his trip go as smoothly as possible.

After poring through more websites, he discovered that there was very little information, if any, on "auditing culture," which came as a bit of a surprise to him. There was information on the audit of the control environment, ethics and code of conduct programs, employee surveys, employee engagement survey, work environment assessment, etc., which are relevant in assessing corporate culture, but nothing that really pulled it together. At the same time, the lack of information provided him with a golden opportunity to help put him and his organisation ahead of everyone else.

His head pounded and he knew he needed to stop or else he would suffer from information overload. He switched his attention to some admin tasks and then breathed a sigh of relief when 5:30 p.m. came and it was time for his commute home. Boy, he needed his run tonight to clear his head. There was much to consider with the task he had taken on.

The starting point of auditing culture is strategy. There is no such thing as a "good" culture, although we do know a fully embedded culture when we see and feel it, as well as one that is aligned to the business goals of the organisation.

Every firm has a culture, and that culture will be defined by its history, location, size, whether it is in a single location, its leadership, and the environment it is operating within. The question is, is it the right culture? And the right culture for what and for whom?

Dr. Allen Zimbler, former chief integration officer (CIO) at Investec Group, wrote the following in the FCA paper DP18/2 Transforming Culture in Financial Services:

> "French and Bell (1978) first proffered the metaphor of an iceberg as a means of describing the difference between those 'harder,' more overt and objective elements of an organisation (its systems, structures, stated strategies, financial control and reporting mechanisms, information technologies, procedures, marketing of products or services, etc.) which were above water level and were definable, measurable, open to inspection and even controllable, and the 'softer,' more covert aspects.

> "These latter properties, inherent in each and every organisation, consist of the perceptions, emotions, attitudes, value systems, interpersonal dynamics, conflicts and even power agendas imported into the organisation by the human beings that inhabit it. And these are, by definition, below the water level of the iceberg, submerged, subjective, irrational, unpredictable, sometimes darker, unmeasurable. But they have a massive impact on an organisation and often subvert the rational, above-the-water-level agenda, sometimes fundamentally."

The right culture for an organisation is one that helps it achieve its business goals, its strategy, and its vision. It has to be right for your particular business. Not only that, but it has to be embedded across every area of the business with a relentless focus from the top.

Grant Thornton's International Business Report (IBR) asked more than 2,500 business leaders across 36 countries what steps their board is taking in relation to the organisation's culture. The number one step being taken by boards in every region is to establish internal controls that address culture and employee behaviour. Nearly three in four boards (71%) are doing this (see **exhibit 1**).

All very interesting. However, when we look at the global statistics and the 71% score for business culture, it does make us ask what business culture actually is: 84% score the conduct of the senior management team as critical, but is this not part of culture; is not the treatment of and relationship with employees and suppliers also business culture? Seeing "culture" as outside of all of these drivers is partly the challenge, not only for Alex and internal audit functions but also for leaders. Culture drivers across the business need to be understood and aligned.

Exhibit 1: Factors Business Leaders Globally See as Most Critical to Reputation/Brand Image

90% Quality of products/services

89% Customer service

84% Conduct of senior management team

80% Treatment of and relationship with employees

80% Financial performance

75% Treatment of and relationship with suppliers

74% Overall mission or sense of purpose

71% Businesses' culture

64% Innovation around products and services

58% Environmental impact of operations

55% Level of diversity in workforce

54% Advertising and communication activities

Source: Grant Thornton's 2017 report Beyond Compliance - the building blocks of strong corporate culture.

Up to 90% of culture programmes fail, and they can fall down at any point along the design and embedding journey. Generally, it is because the culture is not, by design, aligned closely enough with the business strategy, or because one of the culture drivers is not operating effectively, or because the deployment is not even and there is a destructive subculture. There is much that can go wrong, but there is also a clear path to full embedding of culture and to lasting change.

"A strategically relevant culture is vital," says Jennifer Chatman, professor of management at the University of California, Berkeley, Haas School of Business. "A leader's job is to help people develop the ability to make good decisions, judgment calls, and tradeoffs—the ones that leaders would make—that are aligned with strategy."

Once the "what" and the "how" of strategy are defined and agreed, implementation and embedding are critical. And your employees watch whether you mean it every single step of the way.

So how does management implement and embed a culture? Well, there are leadership and management interventions across the organisation at multiple points every single day. Employees subconsciously look for alignment and consistency to the messages and stated culture from the top of the organisation. Leaders who are passionate about their culture and get it right pay attention to, ruthlessly focus on, every part of the organisation and everything the organisation does, not just so it can achieve the strategic goals in terms of what the organisation is doing, but also the culture, how the organisation is going about doing it.

We call these interventions the drivers of culture, the enablers to having a culture that is aligned and consistent with the business goals. If we know what leaders need to focus on across these drivers in order to embed the culture, then as auditors we know what to test in order to successfully audit culture. We need to cover each of the drivers in our audit and test both design effectiveness and operational effectiveness—testing whether it is actually working on the ground across the organisation and across each of the drivers.

So what are these drivers of culture? We have already seen that strategy is a key driver. It is the critical starting point for culture with the purpose of playing a key role in the achievement of business goals. Leadership is also key with leaders across the business and at different levels of leadership, needing to actively and personally engage in the culture going way beyond the traditional tone from the top. People management is a further driver impacting on employees and promoting and encouraging the right behaviours across the organisation. However, the culture drivers do not stop here—the management of other resources, the processes and measures across the organisation, and how change is designed and delivered are also key, as is supply chain management, web presence, external reputation, and communication.

An audit of culture does encompass huge swathes of the organisation and can initially be daunting. However, a structured focus on the design and operational effectiveness of each driver can quickly show areas that are misaligned, inconsistent, and that mean the overall culture is not embedded and enabling the achievement of business goals. **Exhibit 2** shows all of the drivers of culture and gives an overall structure that can help Alex as he embarks on his journey.

Exhibit 2: Drivers of Culture

Strategy

- Business strategy
- Mission
- Vision, values, & behaviours
- Ethics & conduct
- Alignment throughout the organisation

Leadership

- Tone from the top
- Communications consistency
- Role modelling
- Recognising good behaviours
- Treating customers & suppliers fairly

People Management

- Recruitment & retention
- Competence & capability
- Reward & recognition
- Succession planning & talent management
- Performance management

Resource Management

- Supply chain management
- Physical assets
- IT tools/presence
- Financial controls
- Front office/back office
- Third-party service providers, contractors, agents, alliance, partners, & acquired companies
- Marketing materials

Process Management and Change

- Risk management & lines of defence
- Processes critical to culture
- Business policies & standards
- Call scripts & letters
- Welcoming customers
- Transformation

Corporate Responsibility

- Environmental impact
- Sustainability
- External coverage & perception
- Community impact

Key Success Factors

- Clarity of the desired culture and alignment of that culture to the business goals
- Clear articulation of the culture on an ongoing basis so everyone in the organisation understands what it should be

Important Questions

- Is there a written business strategy? If so, does it cover both business goals and culture?
- Does your organisation place as much importance on employees as it does on customers and shareholders?

- Do you believe your leaders are united behind your strategy?

- Does the organisation keep up to speed with competitor and market developments, including cultural aspects?

- Are the values, behaviours, ethics, and conduct requirements clearly communicated to all employees?

- Is your organisation free from unhelpful silos?

- Are you regularly updated about your organisation's success and direction?

Fieldwork – Leadership

On Wednesday morning, Alex woke after a night of interrupted sleep. His run the night before had helped, but when he went to bed, his mind was still whirring and wouldn't let him rest. He kept coming back to how he could successfully come up with a culture audit when he was still unsure of what culture was.

There was only one thing for it. He would have to get out and about and use all his years of audit experience to ask all the right questions, combined with all of his online research for this task. That was his plan. With a new buzz of energy, he strode into his London office ready to go and start talking to people at all levels.

First of all, he logged onto the company intranet and did a search of employees by department. A couple of seconds later, the photo of Kamala and her contact information appeared on his screen. He grabbed his phone and called her.

"Hi, Kamala. It's Alex. You offered your help the other day when our paths crossed. Do you have some time for a quick call later today?"

Kamala was delighted to hear from him, especially as she knew his project had potential to shake things up in the organisation. "Sure," she said. "How about at 11:00 a.m.? I have a 30-minute slot free then."

Alex put the phone down, relieved to have found someone inside the company who could help him. He discovered she had studied people behaviour, cultural differences, and people motivation and had a master's degree in organisational development. She would be perfect to help, and she was someone who seemed keen to be involved.

During his meeting with Kamala, Alex used the time to quiz her on her knowledge of organisations. Whilst listening carefully, he also made sure he took notes that he would reflect on later.

The day sped by and it was the middle of the afternoon when Isobella emailed Alex with all of his travel documentation, the contact information, and schedule of appointments that she had prepared for the next few days.

Tomorrow he would be in Manchester before heading to Glasgow; later next week he would be heading to Amsterdam and New York. He cursed silently to himself. He was making progress, but was it fast enough? All he knew was that the board meeting would not be changed, so he had no option but to get on and do the best he could.

The good news was that the call with Kamala had gone very well and she had left him with much to consider. As he summarised the notes of his call, he jotted down the key points that she mentioned.

There is no right or wrong culture—although there is a right or wrong culture FOR YOU and your strategy. It all comes down to whatever delivers business goals in terms of its objectives. Culture should be owned and managed and not just an accident of history—or of who happens to work there.

The culture of the organisation includes everyone. It's not just people or the leaders but also partners, alliances, acquired companies or M&A targets, third-party service providers, suppliers, indirect customers, etc. Some organisations use brand champions, culture champions, or identify culture carriers to help them embed culture.

Employees watch what happens all the time. They want to know if the organisation really means it in terms of the culture it espouses, or if it will roll over or revert to type when pressure for financial results is on.

Kamala had been a great resource to his work and he had no doubt he would be calling on her again before he was finished. Alex liked Kamala, who was doing a great job in communications in terms of breaking down the old silo mentality that had existed under the previous CEO. Helping overcome silos was an important part of the culture of an organisation, he felt.

Whilst his notes were not exhaustive at this stage, he was jotting it all down and recording conversations. Over the next week or so he was going to speak to many people both inside and outside of his organisation. Then he would be able to pull everything together and join the dots at the end.

The frustration that Alex had was that this task was progressing without him having a full picture of what he was looking for, or the methodology he would use to find it. But he knew that ultimately culture was enterprise critical. There must be a short cut to understanding this, he thought. Someone must be leading the field when it comes to auditing culture, he reasoned. Was there anyone he knew in his network that could help?

And that was when the penny dropped. Of course there was. He should call Sarah.

Sarah had been Alex's mentor since he began his career in auditing. She had helped him get started. As well as being a mine of information, she was very positive and forward thinking. If anyone was going to be a pioneer in the space he was looking at, it would be her. Thank goodness they had remained in touch on LinkedIn. He would send her a message when he got home.

His day continued and he found himself sitting in a senior leadership meeting as an observer. He mentally took a step back and watched the behaviour instead of his normal perspective, which was to listen to the content of the conversation. He recognised that leaders in any organisation play a key role with their people management decisions and wondered what part their consistency, or lack of, impacts on a culture. Whilst listening to the conversation and watching the leaders interact, he considered the business strategy—to really enable it to be realised, the leaders had to work together, had to agree "how" they would achieve those goals, and had to do it together. And not only when they were with each other in meetings but when they left and individually faced their own teams.

As he was leaving the meeting, Sam waved to him to join her at her desk. She was a CEO who wanted to be visible to all her people. The only time she used a closed office was for purely confidential meetings.

"How are you getting on with the challenge I left you on Monday?" she asked.

"It's starting to take shape. I have made some good connections that can help and, for the next week, I am furthering my research by visiting other divisions in this country and overseas," he replied.

"Ok, good. Do let me know if you need anything further from me to help. I have just emailed you a document that sets out our strategy for the next five years and sent you some web links to useful information on organisational culture," she said.

Thanking her, Alex turned and almost collided with Bill.

Bill waited until Sam was out of earshot and view before he told Alex that he thought Alex was wasting time, which could be better spent elsewhere.

"No one cares about culture," he said. "But good luck with it anyway," he smirked.

Bill's comment just helped fuel the fire within Alex to do the best possible job he could and prove Bill wrong.

On returning home, Alex changed into his running gear, grabbed his water bottle, put his headphones on, and started his usual evening run. Still smarting from Bill's comment, he wanted to get himself in a good frame of mind for his chat with Sarah.

Alex knew that Sarah would help him if she was around. Fortunately for Alex, she was available and delighted to catch up with him.

In broad terms, he outlined what he was seeking to do and then he stopped talking. Being a true helper, Sarah volunteered a lot of information. This is what she told him:

"It all starts with strategy and culture and how they work together. If strategy is the 'what,' then culture is the 'how,' and both of these elements need to work in partnership to help the organisation achieve its business goals.

"The achievement of business strategy is so much more difficult if the culture isn't right. So culture is just as important as strategy. It really is the enabler and can unlock all of the organisation's challenges. It takes focus and effort to change culture, but the effort is worth it if the new culture is aligned with the business strategy.

"As you know, organisations have to look at their risk. Historically, financial and operational risks were key, but increasingly now there is a recognition that there is risk associated with culture. In simple terms, if the culture is wrong, then the organisation faces a substantial enterprise-level risk. This can take many forms.

"If I was the CEO, I would want you to show me how the business is controlling the cultural risk. Your role is not to manage the culture. Your role is to verify that it is being owned and managed by the business. You are there to check it is aligned to strategy. You are looking for a consistency of message, behaviour, and values—consistency and alignment are the real keys to the embedding of culture. Without it, unwanted subcultures arise. You will be making a really positive impact on your organisation—culture is a positive enabler for success.

"Alex, you can do this. You have the capability and you are really intuitive with people. I wish you well with your exploration and overseas travels. Do let me know if I can help you further."

He knew he would have to look up the subject of subcultures as that phrase had cropped up a few times during the day and he still didn't know what they were or if they were good or bad. He also wanted to investigate the impact of leadership on culture. What if there was poor leadership or a breakdown of communication? What impact would that have on an organisation having a strong culture?

One thing that kept coming back to him was when Sarah had said, "You need a ruthless focus on culture just as strongly as the way that organisations have a ruthless focus on strategy."

He went to bed feeling good. Wednesday had been a big breakthrough day.

We know that leaders have a key role to play in the culture of the organisation and we hear much about tone from the top, especially from regulators. But how can we audit this? How can we take such a topic as leadership and identify the risks and controls?

Steve Denning, publishing in *Forbes,* noted the following:

"Changing an organization's culture is one of the most difficult leadership challenges. That's because an organization's culture comprises an interlocking set of goals, roles, processes, values, communications practices, attitudes, and assumptions.

"The elements fit together as a mutually reinforcing system and combine to prevent any attempt to change it. That's why single-fix changes, such as the introduction of teams, or Lean, or Agile, or Scrum, or knowledge management, or some new process, may appear to make progress for a while, but eventually the interlocking elements of the organizational culture take over and the change is inexorably drawn back into the existing organizational culture.

"Changing a culture is a large-scale undertaking, and eventually all of the organizational tools for changing minds will need to be put in play."

If this is true for leaders wishing to change a culture, it is also true for leaders who want to maintain their culture every day to ensure they really do achieve their long-term goals. It follows that if that is what leaders need to do, then we in audit can identify the actions they need to take and find audit evidence to support it. Leaders not only need to design a culture that acts as an enabler to business goals, they need to focus their attention on putting it into place—embedding it. Alex was aware of that from his observation of the senior leadership behaviour.

To structure this as auditors, we need to look for evidence of the following;

- A structured design of the culture linked to business strategy
- Regular communication to the whole organisation
- Personal commitment and living of the values
- Actions to embed the culture within the organisation
- Monitoring of the culture over time and across teams/sites/functions
- Reinforcement of the culture with direct reports, at events, etc.

As Larry Senn observed, "Organisations become 'shadows of their leaders.'"

This is at two levels, their own personal behaviour AND obtaining buy-in from others—how they embed across their teams. Both levels are important, and during audits we expect leaders to be able to talk about their personal investment of time, their personal role modelling, and what they do with their teams in terms of recognising positive behavioural contributions from others who help in embedding the culture as well as how they inspire that behaviour in others.

When looking for evidence in terms of leaders' communication, we can also use digital tools. This can range from a relatively straightforward use of computer-aided audit techniques searching communications over a period of time from a number of leaders for references to culture, values, and behaviours, through to more complex sentiment analysis covering not only leaders' communications but blogs, chat rooms, etc. Marketing, product, social media, and political experts have used sentiment analysis for a number of years to understand the subtleties of opinions, their changes over time, and the impact they could have on the organisation.

Sentiment analysis looks at language and text and uses computational linguistics to look at the opinions and changing views in the organisation systematically. It is widely applied in organisations to voice-of-the-customer materials such as reviews and survey responses, online and social media, for applications that range from marketing to customer service to clinical medicine, but there is no reason at all it cannot be used during a culture audit. In fact, it provides data points and trends that can serve as vital evidence as culture or culture change is embedded.

Sentiment analysis can also be useful in assessing the depth of understanding of the values, behaviours, etc., down the organisation, or the consistency of communication by senior leaders either over time or across business lines and functions. It can be especially insightful during a culture change programme in tracking the changes in attitude in large populations over weeks and months, providing insight on the reach of the programme overall and also of the effectiveness of pieces of communication or launch events. Any areas of concern can be picked up on and acted upon very quickly, and successes can be understood and built on in real time.

The approach can sound complex, but business leaders are frequently comfortable in this space and can see the benefit of such analysis, having experienced it with marketing and product launches over a number of years. The use of the outputs and the exploration of these themes in leadership interviews can show both design and operating effectiveness at play across each of the drivers.

What is absolutely vital is that leaders pay real attention to the espoused values and culture. It is the first of the culture drivers where strategic intent around culture can unravel. The first thing employees look for is that leaders know, understand, and role model the values they expect from others. Yet, sometimes this is not the case.

Lucy Kellaway, a columnist at *Financial Times*, demonstrated this common flaw in an experiment with managers from more than 20 companies. She read lists of values from company websites, company by company, and asked the managers to raise their hands when they recognized their own. Only five of the 24 managers responded correctly—and in three cases, it was because they had been on the committees that wrote them. The problem was the extreme degree of overlap in the values, which are often fine words on a page without a living connection through to the strategy.

Key Success Factors

- All leaders actively promoting the consistent and aligned culture

- All leaders role modelling the desired culture

- Having a really simple articulation of the business strategy and the culture and communicating it frequently

Important Questions

- How does the leadership team actively look to add value for customers?

- How does the leadership team develop organisational capability, creativity, and innovation?

- How does the leadership team lead with vision, inspiration, and integrity and role model the required culture?

- Do all of the leadership *equally* role model the required culture, and what actions do each of them take to manage and develop culture?

- Does the senior leadership team actively seek two-way communication with employees, encouraging ideas, contributions, and viewpoints?

- Does the senior leadership team really understand the customer experience?

- Does the senior leadership team understand the culture and what it is like to work in the organisation?

- Does the senior leadership team recognise those who help promote the desired organisational culture?

- Does the senior leadership team ensure that the organisation's strategy, culture, and brand work together seamlessly?

- Does the senior leadership team actively encourage development and learning?

- Does the senior leadership team consider culture to be important as part of due diligence in acquisitions?

On the Road – People Management

The 06:20 West Coast service whizzed Alex from London Euston to Manchester Piccadilly. He arrived in good time for his first visit with the managing director of the North West office.

It was an important meeting as he wanted to understand what value the Manchester leaders were placing on culture. The managing director had been in post for three years and was delivering good profit levels. Alex wondered if this came at any detriment to the employees who worked there.

What surprised him was the enthusiasm he saw from all staff at the branch. His visit hadn't been made public to anyone other than the managing director, and Alex had asked him not to mention it. And whilst the director may have warned his staff, Alex felt as though he was very much being genuinely welcomed. He compared the overall feel to that of the London office. London definitely felt different, but how could he put his finger on it, and did it matter?

What a funny thing it was. Just by walking into the Manchester office, he felt a buzz of energy permeating through the staff that worked there. But why was there an energy and a buzz, and what were the enablers to it? Perhaps if Alex understood what they were, then he would be able to audit them.

The rest of his day flew by. He met all sorts of people and bumped into Julie, the head of HR. He was keen to find out her connection to culture; people were surely a big part of culture. He offered to buy her coffee.

As they sat down, he explained he was now looking at the audit of culture and asked what role HR played in defining and embedding culture at Shapers Ltd. Julie was immediately suspicious. Why were internal auditors even considering asking such questions? Did they not know their place? Alex carefully explained that he could help; that with a different perspective around risk and controls, with different techniques and a different mindset, he could potentially add value. And if he couldn't, then the assurance around her approach had to be helpful, right?

Julie eyed him carefully. She started to talk about the people strategy. How she and her team had taken the business strategy and looked in detail for any people implications, and then worked out how the whole function was going to ensure it delivered on every element in an integrated way. Alex was impressed—it was not what he had expected from what he had heard. He asked her to carry on.

In terms of culture, Julie explained that she had to ensure the people strategy made sure the organisation was ready in terms of people at each step of the strategic journey. So she had to cover every aspect of the employee lifecycle. With recruitment, they needed to ensure the firm's vision and values were not only communicated but also able to be lived by every recruit. When people leave, the exit interviews are carefully constructed so that questions are asked about the culture in the area in which the colleague worked, even if it was not their reason for leaving. Each year objectives were set that included not only "what" people were looking to achieve but "how" they were going to do it. That way, each person had a culture objective and one that would impact their performance review, which would form an honest discussion around both elements. In that way, pay and reward were also linked to culture.

Julie also explained the talent identification process, which looked not only at performance but also at potential. During those discussions, Julie told him that culture was a key part of what was debated. Each senior leader was concerned to promote and develop those that could really ensure the culture was carried into the future and they wanted those individuals to be in the organisation's succession plans.

"You must also meet with David, the head of learning and development," she said. "He can tell you how we build culture into all of our learning programmes. Sorry, but I must run. I must get to my next meeting."

Alex sat musing, he had not figured that people management would have culture so embedded within it. And he had heard really bad things about Julie and HR. How could that be when it was so well-constructed? He needed to find out more.

He carried on his sessions in Manchester and discovered an internal group that was really focussed on the customer and actively used all of the information in surveys, on social media, and in calls to improve the customer experience.

With much information to absorb, he was pleased to finally bid the managing director a fond farewell and head back to his hotel room to order some room service, catch up on his emails, and mark up his "culture exploration" file.

Isobella had left him a voicemail to say that his train from Manchester to Glasgow had been delayed by 30 minutes due to an unexpected shortage of train crew. Other than that, there were no other key issues to worry about.

What was running around in his mind was the well-articulated and holistic conversation with Julie that seemed at odds with what was happening on the ground right across the company. Or at least what he had heard. He needed to think about that further.

Once the organisational strategy and the leadership are aligned with culture, the next vital piece is its full integration into the people management practices of the organisation. It is the methodology by which the culture is nurtured and developed, and done well it can breathe life into the whole organisation.

People management has changed significantly in recent years. What was effectively an administrative function has transitioned into a strategic part of the business.

As HR functions have embraced new technologies, straight-through processing via employee and manager self-service, and electronic data interchange with external bodies, the amount of time spent on administration has fallen substantially. HR functions have therefore turned their attention to adding value strategically, embracing analytics and artificial intelligence, and developing integrated programmes to ensure the organisation has the right people with the right skills in the right place at the right time. World-class, leading edge HR functions have turned themselves into true business partners.

In order to achieve this, the organisational model used by the vast majority of HR functions is called the Ulrich model, identified and then developed by Dave Ulrich of the University of Michigan. In its simplest form, it divides the remaining administrative side of HR from the policy centres of excellence—Learning and Development, Talent,

Resourcing, Organisation Design, Performance and Reward, and Employee Relations—from both the remaining operational and administrative side. Most significantly, it also provides strategic business partners who look at business strategy and culture and focus on adding long-term value utilising the centres of excellence as a resource.

This is all well and good, but what significance does this have in terms of culture and the active management and ownership of it that is so important? Well, the business partners should have identified, either for the whole business or for a part of it, what the people strategy is and ensure that HR as a function plays a key part in ensuring it is realised.

So what does the HR team need to do in order to ruthlessly embed the culture across the organisation? If we follow the employee lifecycle, then the employer brand should be designed to include the values and behaviours so that it is clear to potential employees what the culture of the organisation is, or should be. Then the interview process should include questions to test it. This is not about recruiting clones or a lack of diversity—there are many ways to fit into a culture and many skills and talents to bring to it, but a fit with values is important.

Once recruited, objectives need to be set that not only include "what" an individual needs to do but also "how:" how they behave with colleagues, what conduct is expected, etc. Then at each performance assessment, the "how" can be discussed and assessed. This does need managers with the capability to have honest conversations and to have evidenced examples of aligned and non-aligned behaviour. But what it also does is make the culture matter right across the business and enable great examples to be gathered and communicated more widely. Use of storytelling in this way can further illustrate what the organisation values, what it is looking for in terms of behaviour, and give others the confidence to both reflect the desired behaviours and to speak up when the values and behaviours are not aligned.

Once the culture is built into the performance review cycle, it can then be used to inform promotion discussions. Promotion interviews and capability frameworks should both include behaviours and values. It will be vital to the organisation to have the leaders and managers of the future able to achieve its business goals over the long term. It can be used in talent assessment—either directly as a measure or included in the performance measurement. Then from the talent pool, succession plans can be drawn for senior role succession that will ensure the culture endures over the life of the business strategy and beyond.

Through all of this, learning programmes can be developed that reflect the values and behaviours needed. Then right from induction through to senior manager training, values and behaviours can be reflected in the content or added as specific modules depending on the need and the degree of change needed.

Whilst looking at the topic of people management, one of the real pitfalls with auditing culture is the ease with which the auditor can slip back into a functional or topic-based audit. With people management in particular, it is really easy to slip into an HR audit—looking at risk and controls across the function. This is not your purpose here.

An HR audit looks at the risks and controls, looks for a well-governed function, and looks at whether the function is doing things right. The people management element of a culture audit looks at whether the function is doing the right things.

But how can auditors be the judge of whether they are doing the right things? Surely that is not their role. Our answer lies in going back to the business strategy, looking at the defined culture, and looking at whether the people strategy is really tied in to that, and then the whole programme of activity across the function—and into the business—is consistently aligned. If it is, then they are doing the right things.

To summarise, **exhibit 3** highlights the areas we would typically consider in both an HR audit *and* in the people management area of a culture audit. With both, we need to be careful as to where the risk and controls lie—in the HR function or in the business. With modern HR functions, the risk and controls lie across both, as the implementation of straight-through processing and such things as performance management and talent identification have moved the risk and therefore the controls across to the business.

Key Success Factors

- Aligning all elements of people management to the desired culture and ruthlessly focussing on the "how"
- Having a people strategy aligned to the business strategy enabling embedding of the culture across the organisation
- Making culture matter in performance management, appointments, reward, promotions, and engagement actions

Important Questions

- Does the performance management system recognise both the achievement of objectives (the "what") and the behaviours used in their achievement (the "how")?

Exhibit 3: Components of People Risk

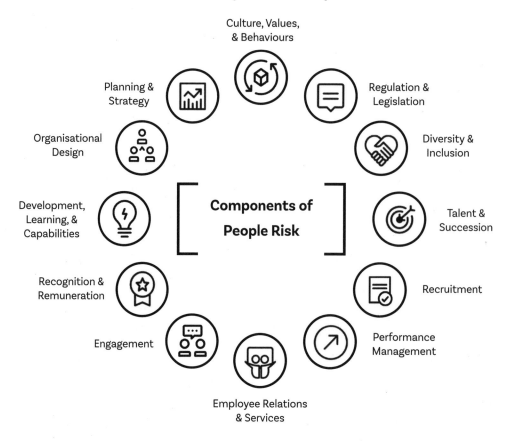

- How does HR use the defined culture in setting policies and working practises?

- Are employees actively engaged in developing and promoting the organisational culture?

- Do the recognition and reward processes and policies have elements that consider an individual's contribution (or otherwise) to culture?

- Does the recruitment process consider culture when looking at new hires?

- Do you feel an important part of the organisation and understand how your job contributes to the overall success?

- When looking for someone new to join your organisation, are behaviours and values taken into account?

- Are action plans created and acted upon following employee surveys?

- Are you encouraged to help develop or promote the organisational culture?

- Does your pay and bonus focus you on the longer term?

- Do the succession planning and talent management discussions include reference to culture?

- Does the training you undertake reflect and encourage the right behaviours and values?

- Does the organisation's capability framework align to the desired culture?

- When people are promoted, do you think the organisation considers their behaviour and values as well as technical capabilities?

Scotland and Local Reputation

Stepping off the rail platform at Glasgow Central, an icy blast cut through Alex. Shivering, he took a taxi and headed away from the centre on his journey to meet with Simon, the deputy director of the Scottish division. He wondered what kind of reception he would receive when he got to the office—what kind of culture he would feel.

As he arrived, he noticed that the office looked different, the notice boards, the layout, and screen savers all carried different messages. He asked Simon about this, who told him that on the whole the office was pretty self-sufficient and didn't need much in the way of guidance or resources from the head office in London. As he made his coffee in the kitchen, there was no negative chat about the London office (maybe that was because he was based there), but he did wonder what the impact on culture was of such a different feel to an office. Alex would speak to Kamala about it later on to get her view of it from a communications perspective.

Alex really enjoyed meeting the staff and understood what they were doing in the division. It actually had more energy than the Manchester office—and that was saying something. Simon had arranged for Alex to sit in on a couple of staff focus groups which were discussing the recent employee survey and aiming to arrive at actions to make improvements. Alex was interested to see how they ran and was impressed by the open and honest feedback that was given. All the staff seemed to know they would be listened to and felt the feedback would be followed up on.

Whilst in Glasgow, Alex was also told about the charity initiatives that the office had carried out. As he was a runner and as some of the fundraising had been through taking part in various marathons in the UK and Europe, he was very interested and listened avidly as the staff told him about their training and the race itself.

He remembered Sarah's thoughts on corporate responsibility at work and culture. She had said, "Corporate responsibility is a culture driver, it forms part of your external reputation, and it is not just about charitable giving but also about sustainability, impact on your environment, and investor and media relations. All of this should be aligned with your business objectives. It is important how you express your organisation to the external community. Employees watch what you do and subconsciously look for alignment between your external messaging and the internal reality of working there."

With those words ringing in his ears, Alex wondered whether the Glasgow office had considered this when it came to its external activities and reputation. When he asked Simon about it, he was told that they received very little in the way of support from head office and so had decided at the local management meeting what they would do in terms of press, local sponsorship, and charitable giving.

Simon was aware of the Shapers Ltd. Charitable Giving Policy, but he had no support from head office. Rather than do nothing, he had decided on his own activities.

Alex wondered about the impact of this and guessed that Sarah, if asked, would have said something along the lines of "it all depends on the alignment to your business goals," or words to that effect. She was certainly a pioneer in this cultural field, and Alex was so pleased that he could ask her some more.

From his wider reading, Alex knew that many millennials place great importance on company corporate responsibility when looking at prospective employers. Sustainability and wider environmental concerns were key factors, almost as much as salary, benefits, and work-life balance. He was starting to see the connections between leadership, people management, corporate responsibility, and reputation—and how they had to work together.

He wondered how corporate responsibility activities also helped the brand and awareness of his company. After all, these projects would mean interaction with all sorts of people, including the public, suppliers, stakeholders, and others. Could a single project damage the brand? One thing he also knew was that suppliers, customers, investors, other employees, etc., as well as potential recruits, are making judgements all the time. They are effectively scanning what is going on with an organisation and with the internet and social media. Anything that was an issue or a challenge would firstly be known fast and secondly very easily through searches. What they are doing is making assessments as to whether what the organisation says it does and what it actually does are in alignment or not.

Alex felt that the more he delved into his cultural auditing quest, the more he was becoming fascinated by it—by both the topic itself and the holistic approach needed across the organisation.

Following his catch-up with Julie yesterday, he decided to ask a few questions about HR and how it linked into the local business. After what he had heard from Julie, he thought the approaches would really be adding value. He sought out a couple of people managers after the focus groups and quizzed them. He was surprised to find they were quite scathing about HR at Shapers. They reported a lack of support with recruitment, a system that was challenging to work with, difficulties with booking their employees on courses, and an overall feeling that they were now doing HR's job for them with all the inputting they needed to do in the system. "What do they actually do over there?" one of them said. Alex was shocked. While he knew he also spent time on the HR system with his own department, he also remembered filling in forms for "personnel" that no longer needed to be done. He quizzed them further, exploring the resourcing process and the learning process and finding out where the bottlenecks were. His questioning found controls that were not working and processes that were broken. He made notes of all of it that he would write up later.

The focus groups that he had sat in on while in Glasgow were so effective in obtaining feedback around the operational effectiveness of culture that when he returned to London, he pulled together another. He decided that to lead these sessions as part of his methodology of testing whether the culture on the ground—and how it was perceived at more junior levels—was as the leaders intended it to be and the best way to go. His sample was the attendees themselves, with a mix of experiences, tenure, grades, and ages. He had found that using storytelling was a really great way to get people to open up about the culture. He kept it anonymous and genuinely did not know who said what by the time he had undertaken a few. He found that the stories he was told fit beautifully into the culture drivers.

Reputation and its constituent parts, including corporate responsibility, is a key area of focus for many organisations now. In terms of culture, it is a part of ensuring that the culture is managed holistically by the senior leadership in alignment with the business strategy.

Reputation is critical for any business and for its culture. Employees, future employees, clients, customers, and other stakeholders all make judgements about an organisation's culture by looking at it from the outside. If the culture is aligned to the business strategy and managed and owned across all of the culture drivers, then what people will see externally will look connected, have less negative social media comment, have fewer complaints, and will look like a working connected whole.

So for us as auditors, we must consider the external reputation and how the organisation manages it. There is a plethora of information available via internet searches with press coverage available, but also in many countries there is feedback and scores from both current and prior employees.

In January 2018, Larry Fink, founder of the world's largest investment firm, BlackRock, wrote this to CEOs of the companies in which he invests:

> "Society is demanding that companies, both public and private, serve a social purpose. To prosper over time, every company must not only deliver financial performance, but also show how it makes a positive contribution to society. Companies must benefit all of their stakeholders, including shareholders, employees, customers, and the communities in which they operate."

Fink was right. However, it is not only the purpose of the organisation that is key here, it is also a piece of the culture jigsaw. It goes towards making culture a seamless whole, tied together beautifully, making it come alive for all stakeholders, both internal and external. Investor relations, reputation, and community affairs can be managed by a number of departments across the organisation, and indeed is rarely managed from a single team. This means that an aligned design is critical—sending a connected view to external parties and also ensuring that operating effectiveness across sites, functions, and topics as varied as job adverts to product launches and sponsorships is an important part of an aligned message.

In this part of Alex's journey, we also start to see the difference in other drivers between the design effectiveness of culture and the operational effectiveness. With culture, as with other audit topics, both are critical in terms of managing the overall risk. Alex was starting to uncover some of the difference through his discussions on HR. Whilst

Julie was able to explain all of the theory of the employee value proposition and associated employee lifecycle from a culture perspective, that message was not felt inside the organisation. It was an empty promise for the users of those services and did not add what value it could to the wider culture of the organisation.

As auditors we need to find a way to test both, and we will explore how we can do this over the following chapters. One is to have tests for both approach *and* deployment; the other is to utilise storytelling around culture from groups of individuals to look into what works in practice and what doesn't. Alex had started to discover the positive benefits of this testing approach and build it into his approach going forward.

Key Success Factors

- Pay attention to your external reputation as employees watch for alignment with internal culture messaging.

- This reputation could be via media, web presence, or even via relationships with activist or environmental groups, depending on your business. Employees watch and reflect on alignment with internal messages.

Important Questions

- Does your organisation support charitable work and does it align with your culture?

- Does your website reflect the organisation's culture?

- Does your intranet reflect and actively promote your culture?

- Is external media monitored and managed—as far as it can be—to help support the reputation of the organisation and its culture?

- When you see your organisation's name in a headline, do you expect the article to be positive?

Overseas Travel Beckons – Resource Management

After Glasgow, Alex returned to his home on Friday evening. He couldn't quite believe that it had only been Monday when the subject of culture and how to audit it had been mentioned. Now he felt as though he was beginning to make sense of it. A run for him was definitely in order—further this time, as a celebration of the progress he had made.

Tomorrow, being Saturday, he planned to leave the day to play itself out. He had no plans other than to chill and then pack a bag for his overseas trips to the Netherlands on Sunday and New York a few days later. It really was a full-on time for him, but he had to keep progressing with his cultural exploration.

Following the short flight to Schipol on Sunday and a good night's sleep at a local hotel, he met Nils, the regional director in Amsterdam, and asked to meet the employees in a similar focus group to the ones he had held in the UK. Alex was getting into the swing of them now. However, Nils told him that in the Netherlands, most of the Shapers work was outsourced and there were only a few people in the central office in Amsterdam.

This took Alex by surprise, as he didn't quite realise that this was how Shapers worked in the central European countries. In the overall risk assessment, they had always come out as low risk in the assessment of auditable entities, and so the audit cycle had not reached them during his tenure at Shapers. He wondered what this meant for culture and how he could audit it. He would need to reflect on that one.

What he was able to do was log on to the company intranet and do a search for culture and each one of the values and see what came up. It was an interesting selection of articles, but he was not sure if they told the whole story of culture at Shapers—not only as it was, but neither how Shapers wanted it to be. He wondered what the outside world saw and so he typed in www.shapers.com and waited to see what came up. The familiar logos and pictures of the products soon showed themselves and Alex spent a good hour clicking his way around the site with an outsider's eye, looking at the story it told him about the culture.

The annual report and accounts laid out the strategy, and a word search showed mention of the values and approach. There was a very well-worded piece on employees, which Alex knew Julie would have written. It gave a real clear articulation of the people strategy and the role it would play in the organisation's future, but he didn't think any area gave a real feel for the culture.

On his way back to the hotel, Alex reflected that all of the resources the company had at its disposal needed to be aligned to the culture and made a note to talk to procurement when he got back to London. Did they select outsourced suppliers on price, quality, or some other measure? And if they were taking on outsourced providers who would talk directly to customers as they did in the Netherlands, were the measures different? Did they ask about the suppliers' own culture or do any checks for alignment with that of Shapers? Alex could clearly see the risks in the supply chain from a culture perspective and, from his time on the intranet and the web, he could see how it would be beneficial to align them behind the culture too. He also reflected that if Shapers were to acquire another company, how important it would be to understand not only the financials and the strategy of the acquired company but also the culture.

It had been another good day with another piece of the jigsaw. It wasn't all about leadership and people, there were other elements at play too. That evening Alex went to a football game. He wasn't normally a supporter, but he decided he would take in the game between Ajax and PSV Eindhoven. It wasn't the most thrilling game he had ever seen. Ajax won 1-0 in the end, but it was a slow game for the neutral supporter. What struck Alex though, given the culture lessons running around in his head, was how the team had different roles and how it didn't come together as a performance unless everyone contributed. There had to be high capability, a purpose, a relentless focus on the task in hand, a recognition of handover points between team players, and every position had to play its part. Maybe it was the same with culture, that it wouldn't really work properly, come alive, unless each piece was in place. That was something to ponder on. He was wondering what he would learn in New York.

Resource Management

When looking to audit culture, strategy, leadership, and people are important, but they are not the only things impacting the culture, or indeed the reputation, of the organisation. External web presence, internal intranet, supplier selection and management, management information—in terms of what is measured—as well as the look and feel of office buildings all play a part in building a holistic and managed culture. Leaders with a strong culture pay attention to all aspects where people, whether current or potential employees, customers, investors, and other external stakeholders, receive messages from or form opinions about the organisation.

So how can you actively manage these other aspects? Procurement is a key team to engage with in terms of their process and selection methodologies. How do they measure success—cost savings or brand alignment? Each could lead to very different suppliers in terms of both selection and ongoing management. Each organisation needs to consider what this third-party usage of brand message means for them. For Shapers, it is suppliers contracted to provide services. For an insurance company, it could be a third-party network of independent financial advisors dealing with customers where it is the advisors that have the main relationship with the client and the organisation is merely the product provider. But if that product doesn't perform, whose reputation suffers? Whose culture is impacted? What if those advisors are chasing returns for themselves rather than what is best for the customer? And whose reputation will suffer if the best advice is not given? Third parties can therefore be a complex area on their own in terms of culture, and audit needs to look at both the third-party risks, the design of third-party selection methodologies, and the measures of success in order to assess design effectiveness alone.

As for operating effectiveness, feedback from third parties, any supplier surveys, complaints, compliments, and the view of any internal handoff party are all valuable sources of information. What is really important to remember is that this is a culture audit and not a procurement audit. It is very easy to start looking at procurement and third parties and slip into a risk and control audit of the function itself and not an assessment of the impact on culture. It is important to set out the risks and controls of this area with respect to culture before beginning testing in order to mitigate the risks of the audit results not being related to culture.

In addition to third parties and measures, spending time testing what the outside world sees in relation to the culture of the organisation is also important. It can provide a valuable source of testing—not just in terms of the resources driver but also in terms of reputation. There are many sites on the web that give a picture of the organisation in terms of customer and employee feedback—including the organisation's own website—and we in audit do not often spend enough time assessing them.

With a culture audit, they can be a real source of operational effectiveness assessment and provide specific and measureable feedback. As with any feedback, we need to place it in an overall context, ensure the sample is helpful, and assess for the self-selection of samples, such as those on the "glass door." It does not mean the sample cannot be used, care just needs to be taken with the feedback—and any feedback may need further testing internally before inclusion in the final report. The information gleaned, however, can be crucial in assessing the overall culture of the organisation, as clues may be apparent that are not visible internally and it can clearly show areas for further testing.

Before completing "resource management," a feel for the office environment can also provide evidence. What is the layout, what are the seating arrangements, who gets an office (if anyone), what does the kitchen space look like, and, in particular, what is displayed on notice boards? For one organisation we audited, the front office was sparkling, clean, and welcoming, and yet the back office was full of stationary boxes, Christmas decorations, stained coffee mugs, and other assorted clutter. The cultural read from employees on this one? Customers matter and we don't!

Key Success Factors

- An understanding that culture reaches into the supply chain
- Active ownership of the communications via internet and intranet and ruthless alignment to the culture
- Careful management of work environments to ensure alignment to culture

Important Questions

- Does the design of offices and/or customer space actively reflect your culture? (Think about the meeting spaces, the look and feel, notice boards, kitchen areas, etc.)
- Does your organisation's marketing materials reflect your organisation's culture?
- Does your organisation treat its suppliers fairly?
- When tendering for suppliers, does the organisation look at culture and how the supplier would contribute to or fit with the organisation's own culture?

Coffee in Times Square – Process and Transformation

The next day, Alex was on a direct flight to JFK from Amsterdam and used the opportunity to write up his notes and do some thinking around culture as an issue. He had realised that as with other audits, a culture audit is a snapshot, a point in time, and that culture is a living, moving thing with many influences on it. He had also realised that there was no such thing as a single culture for an organisation to aspire to. What it needed was a healthy culture, and one that helped it achieve its business goals. He nodded off for half an hour and then when food was being served, he decided to watch a film. None of the latest releases appealed to him, so he flicked through the back catalogue and decided to watch *Erin Brockovich*, which he'd missed the first time around. As the story progressed, he noticed the link with the organisation culture and the devastation it caused for the company, its employees, and the communities in which it resided. Of course, he realised it wasn't just about charitable giving. It was about the reputation of the organisation and its sustainability, and not just in terms of environmentally friendly tuna in the canteen but the very heart of ensuring a long-term future of the organisation for the benefit of all stakeholders. That was the culture driver here. That's what needed examining. The risks were enormous—enterprise risk—and the controls should have been there; not just from a waste perspective but from the culture and reputation of the organisation.

Arriving in New York with another piece of the jigsaw, he headed to the hotel for a shower and some food. He needed to keep himself awake to readjust his body clock. Walking through the city, it was louder and more frantic than London with an altogether busier feel. People were running from meeting to meeting and shouting into their mobiles as they went. It might run on the same language, but this was a different business culture. Would that have an impact, he wondered.

He was up bright and early the next morning and headed to the office. He wanted to see as much of the operation as he could. He was surprised at the number of people in the office so early and realized he could start his introductions even before 8:00 a.m. He met with Chuck, the regional director, and asked if he could shadow a couple of meetings before his booked focus groups in the afternoon. Chuck was very happy with this so they headed off for a meeting with the IT and sales team to talk about some recent challenges with the client take-on process following a recent transformation programme.

The meeting was really interesting. It was a straightforward discussion around the challenges with the new computer system—around a process that was critical to the customer. Everyone was straight into their understanding of the problem and keen to find a resolution. Alex asked whether the transformation programme itself had considered the impacts on culture as part of its governance. A major programme having impacts on employees, customers, and suppliers would impact culture in some way on implementation. Had they considered whether that impact would be positive and aligned with the business goals, behaviours, and values of the organisation, or had they not discussed it at all? Chuck looked at him thoughtfully and said, "Do you know, Alex. I don't believe we did. We were focused on the task and the system."

Alex reflected over a coffee. If a culture was to be owned and managed by leaders, and large changes were planned, they needed to consider the impacts of the change on culture and potentially use the change as an inflection point if culture changes were needed, or as a way to embed an existing culture further. What a great point in time to do it, when you also had the attention and time of the leaders in terms of input as well as a structure of a steering committee and working parties to utilise. If the discussions started early on in the programme lifecycle, the values and behaviours could be embedded and reinforced, as well as deliver a great new approach. Employees and customers would see an aligned culture and the links between what the leaders were saying, what was written in the strategy documents and on the intranet, and what was really being delivered on the ground. That was when the culture would be reinforced and really come alive.

Alex chatted it through with Chuck who agreed that not only would it be a better approach, it might have actually prevented the problems the client had experienced over the last few weeks. The conversation led to a debate around other processes. There were some client processes that were really critical to how the culture of the business was perceived both internally and externally, ones that were the differentiator for Shapers versus the competition. The process owners would really benefit from considering not only what those processes were delivering for clients, but also how the values fitted into the way they were delivered. Alex wondered whether to do a customer focus group as well as employee focus groups and made a note to ask marketing whether that was in fact something that was undertaken. If so, could he sit in and observe?

When auditing culture, a number of organisations look at leadership and people. Culture is all about people, right? Well yes it is, but in a fully owned and managed culture, the leaders pay attention to everything the organisation is doing. They look at what is measured, at processes and resources, and pay particular attention to the impact of change on the culture.

Much organisational attention is paid to transformation, programme management, and change. Rightly so. Transformation programmes eat a lot of management time and frequently a lot of budget. What is often missing is consideration of the impact of change on the culture of the organisation. Change programmes are often a huge opportunity to reinforce or nudge the culture to bring it more into alignment with the business goals. However, they can equally be a crunch point of disaster—delivering cost savings or making other efficiencies—and in doing so wreaking untold damage on the culture of the organisation that will sometimes take years to overcome.

So how to avoid this and how to audit it? Well-governed programmes will have sponsors, steering committees, agreed terms of reference, working parties covering each element, and frequent—often colourful—reporting. Questioning about the impact the programme will have on the culture once the project is delivered, however, can often lead to blank expressions. Yet, thought given to this at an early stage can almost always lead to better communications, better integration, and a better overall delivery. As auditors, especially if we are undertaking business monitoring and a continuous approach as the programme evolves, we can ask these questions and prompt a holistic look back to the values and behaviours in the business strategy and prompt consideration of the impacts of delivery, and not just the delivery itself. Acknowledging the risk to culture at the stage of writing the risk control matrix and ensuring the controls around culture are included in the transformation audit plan can lead to useful conversations and findings for the business, which can lead to real and significant improvements to the programme itself.

In terms of processes, employees in their scanning of the organisational environment will spot the processes that jar with behaviours and values, where potentially the organisation is looking to put short-term profit before the long-term goals. If these processes are promoted or even tolerated by leaders, the interpretation by employees will be that "you don't really mean it" in terms of the messages around overall culture, and no amount of communications, events, or videos will be able to overcome this. So for an insurance company hiding behind rules to reduce accepted claims, or a bank trying to lengthen the clearing cycle, or a store running down stock at the period ends to customer detriment or complicating special offers, employees will know and will make interpretations of the leaders' buy-in and ownership of culture.

Between resources and processes, management information that is paid attention to by the leaders of the organisation will often tell a story. Is it monthly or quarterly profit, or is it customer or client feedback? Is it around one stakeholder group at the expense of others, as opposed to all stakeholder groups being considered in a balanced scorecard?

We saw a real-life example of this with the research of Professor Linda Treviño, Penn State University, Smeal College of Business – Organizational Behaviour Ethics, Niki A. den Nieuwenboer, The University of Kansas, and João Vieira da Cunha, IÉSEG School of Management:

> "Our research studied a new desk sales unit in a large telecommunications firm, where one member of our team spent 15 months observing how middle managers induced unethical behaviour in their subordinates. Our team member observed formal and informal meetings, interviewed employees, and had access to emails and other company documents. The subordinates, desk salespeople, were brought in to sell smaller telecom products over the phone, allowing the company's higher paid field salesforce to focus on larger sales. This saved the company money and helped ensure smaller sales were profitable.

> "The multi-level process that we uncovered begins with top management who set difficult-to-achieve goals. Middle managers, who were incentivised based upon their subordinates' goal performance, found that their subordinates were unable to reach those goals for several reasons. However, middle managers didn't push back against the goals handed down. Instead, they creatively searched for what we call 'structural vulnerabilities,' which are places in the overall performance structure of the organisation that can be exploited to create

and conceal fake performance. In our research, middle managers coerced subordinates, mostly through shaming practices, to engage in multiple behaviours that made it appear as if goals were being met when they were not. We discuss some of these below. Senior management ended up making important strategic decisions based upon the unit's deceitful performance. Essentially, they were flying blind, without good information about the unit's performance. Our research is important because it surfaces this essential middle manager role. It also highlights how goal-setting in organisations can contribute to unethical behaviour. And, it contradicts research suggesting that employees are often unaware of the ethical implications of their behaviour. Front-line employees in our study were ethically aware, and they resisted the unethical behaviour despite powerful incentives pressuring them to engage in it.

"Most organisations use goal-setting for a very simple reason—it is a powerful and effective performance management tool. Long-established goal-setting research, taught to decades of management students, says that specific, difficult-to-achieve goals are highly motivating. However, research also says that goals that employees deem to be unreachable (for whatever reason) are not motivating and that employees will give up on trying to reach them. Our study revealed a very different angle on this long-held knowledge claim.

"The front-line employees that we studied did think their sales and 'sales work' (number of calls made, etc.) goals were unachievable. Many did not feel knowledgeable enough to be effective at selling products, and the training they received did not resolve this problem. They believed that senior management expected them to do too much sales administrative work. They also complained that the management information system was onerous and absorbed too much time. So, front-line employees were inclined to give up on their performance goals. But their supervisors, middle managers, did not give up on the goals at all. As noted above, middle managers' incentive packages were tied to goal achievement by their direct reports. So rather than allowing employees to give up, middle managers got creative and coerced employees to fake performance in multiple ways. They searched for 'structural vulnerabilities' in the organisation's performance system that allowed them to make it look as if employees were achieving the goals even if they were not, creating a false representation of performance that was reported to senior management. For example, middle managers changed rules such as expanding the definition of 'sales calls' so that more types of behaviours counted toward their sales work goals (e.g., internal calls and emails could count as external sales calls). They also changed salespeople's roles. Amongst others, they instructed their direct reports to adopt an IT administrator role and to propose to the salespeople from the field salesforce (who targeted the same customers) to take over their sales administration. In return, they would get credit for field salespeople's smaller sales that desk salespeople could claim toward their own sales targets despite having little to no involvement in the sale. Middle managers also instructed salespeople on how to make the data flow in the IT system look 'normal.' For example, when logging an order, which did not count toward their sales goals, as a sale, which did, managers instructed direct reports to let a few days pass between opening and closing the order in the IT system, as sales also almost never happened in a single day. Middle managers even developed queries to search the IT system for orders that could be claimed as sales. Finally, middle managers created informal reinforcement mechanisms (especially shaming mechanisms) to coerce subordinates to comply. For example, whiteboards were used to publicly display employees' performance from highest to lowest.

"All of this, plus the fact that many employees did not believe that they had better job options elsewhere, contributed to employees' ultimate submission to middle management's pressures."

From a culture perspective, the more complex the measurement system, the more this kind of behaviour is likely to be prevalent. It is not poor conduct by an individual, it is a normal human reaction to what they perceive as an unfairly designed "system" but one which they feel unable to challenge either because of the impact on their career in the short term or even by a loss of position, which will have wider implications for family, etc.

The responsibility for the measurement system and the process is in the design of the "system" by senior leaders. A further example of this is explained by Dr. Celia Moore, Associate Professor and Academic Fellow, Ethics and Compliance Initiative, Department of Management and Technology, Bocconi University:

"At Wells Fargo, salespeople were assigned a goal of selling eight products to each customer (independent directors of the board of Wells Fargo & Company, 2017). This number was chosen, apparently, because 'eight' rhymed with 'great' (Levine, 2016). Compensation and bonuses were tied to employees meeting this numeric target. And it worked, even though those products were often unwanted and were 'sold' to customers unknowingly. This is because when specific, challenging, numeric goals are set for us, we tend to neglect other priorities while meeting them. This phenomenon is known as 'goal shielding' (Shah, Friedman, & Kruglanski, 2002). In the case of Wells Fargo, the 'eight is great' goal shielded employees from considering the ethical implications of opening accounts that clients neither wanted nor knew about."

What we can clearly see with these examples is that resource usage, processes, measurement, and transformation can have as much impact on the culture of an organisation as the leadership, communication, and people management. Therefore, as auditors, we need to ensure it is covered, both at risk assessment stage and in audit planning and design. If we ignore these areas, we miss much of what makes up an organisation's culture, and with any missing piece, the full culture will not be understood or properly audited.

Key Success Factors

- An understanding of the impact of the measures across the business, both financial and nonfinancial, especially from the perspective of impact on individuals
- Management of processes from a culture perspective to ensure alignment
- For every change or transformation programme, a clear understanding and regular discussion as to the impact of the change on the culture of the organisation when it is implemented

Important Questions

- How does the organisation go about developing, designing, and refining products, and how is customer feedback and other feedback data utilised?
- How does the organisation assess its service in the context of its defined culture?
- Are customer survey results compared to other similar companies, and are actions taken to improve the results?
- Are complaints and compliments that are captured analysed and acted upon?
- Is culture impact a key consideration and measure of success when change is being designed or implemented?
- Do your written policies, procedures, and workflows help you to represent your organisation's culture to your customers?
- Do you know which of your customer-facing processes really matter to your customers?

- Are you comfortable that processes you are asked to follow do not compromise your beliefs and values?

- Is culture recognised as a key risk, and are controls embedded in the risk control framework?

- How do the current measures or management information captured across the organisation help it to understand culture and, significantly, are there any gaps?

- Do you think your organisation treats customers fairly?

Return to London – Working Cross Culture

A few days later, Alex was back in his London office. He had been to Amsterdam and New York, and in that time he had seen how some of the Shapers' overseas offices worked. He had also met a number of their suppliers and customers. He had been involved in all sorts of conversations, attended a number of meetings, and been taken out to dinner by divisional managers. In short, he had met a lot of people, and each time he was able to explore the issue of their culture and their understanding of what impact it had on their business performance.

Kamala rang and asked him what had stood out in terms of country differences to the UK way of working. She was interested in knowing more. "How did you get people to open up and share their ideas with you?" she asked.

Alex glanced out of his window as he reflected on her question and said, "I asked them to tell me two real-life stories about their experience of the culture of the company and then they just spoke from the heart. All sorts of issues came out, some good and some bad, but they were happy to share. I felt privileged that they trusted me with some of their concerns."

Kamala asked if Alex felt that she could work with him to help maximise some of his findings and share them through their communications channels. Alex agreed and made another note in his journal that would be hugely helpful in terms of management actions.

Checking his calendar he realised that he was just in time for his conference call with Clara from the Shanghai office. Isobella had set the call up to provide Alex with another different country culture perspective. Clara was the regional director for China and was happy to give Alex some time. He quizzed her on the culture of Shapers in Asia, and she carefully considered her answers and made sure to cover every point that was asked. She was reticent in sharing the things that were not working so well, but if Alex probed, she was very forthcoming. She understood that culture and strategy were reliant on each other, and from the way she talked about other organisations and their "face," brand, and culture, it was almost as if they had human characteristics. For her, Shapers itself was positive, it was forward looking, but it was also humble and self-effacing, placing more importance on the customer than the organisation or its employees.

Its history in the region was important as was other people's perception of it when you were an employee. Reputation was key. Alex asked her about the impact that would have on leadership and whether the organisational culture would need to be different to reflect what was important to the people. Clara told him the culture didn't need to change, but care needed to be taken with country cultures. Local leaders were constantly interpreting and translating messages from the head office in order to have them resonate locally. They had gotten used to it and could really make it work. Some leaders coming in from other cultures also had an ability to do this, but some didn't. It would be easy to obtain the full buy-in of employees and have them committed to the culture, but it would also be easy to turn them off completely. There was a balance in terms of representing the organisational culture and being respectful of the country culture, and good leaders, whether local or otherwise, intuitively understood that and found a way to marry the two without giving way on the core of either. She wasn't sure how they did that though, and did see a number of leaders who came in not understanding it and not lasting very long.

She gave Alex the example of a sales campaign designed in the head office that they were asked to run. She knew it was too direct and would not work locally, so she asked to tweak it. Once she had, the results were better than in other locations and, in fact, others had picked up on some of her changes and used them to really good effect elsewhere.

Alex came away from the call feeling thoughtful. His overseas trip had produced a completely different feeling than the one that he had from his call with the Shanghai office. He decided that he needed perspective and messaged Sarah to see if she was available for a chat over the weekend. She was, and they agreed to Skype late Sunday morning.

When working with culture, it is important to understand that there are ranges of behaviour within cultures, both within organisational cultures and across countries. Whilst an organisation will have defined vision, values, behaviours, etc. in line with its business goals, there are obviously different characters and personalities as well as motives, levels of capabilities, and so forth, so this can be a challenge for an auditor. Where *do* the bounds of tolerance lay, and where *should* they lay in order to ensure an owned and managed culture? We have seen Alex visit a number of countries and observe the culture portrayed in different ways, and wonder whether this is an issue.

Marketers have worked with a similar problem for a number of years—how to portray global brands in a way that maintains the core of the brand but resonates and therefore "sells" in local markets. Brands that have an Asian humility as part of their character but need to appeal to customers and "sell" in downtown Manhattan. There have been some ingenious campaigns in this kind of arena. HSBC once took a billboard in Times Square and had a booth on the square so the image projected on to the billboard was the customer's own picture alongside the brand, neatly maintaining a customer first brand with humility and its positioning in the heart of New York City.

But what does this tell us in terms of auditing culture? How can we understand the underlying country culture in order to both undertake our fieldwork and ensure our interpretation of responses are correct?

In 1998, management consultants Trompenaars and Hampden-Turner published their Seven Dimensions of Culture model to help explain national cultural differences in organisations and show how managing these differences is a real challenge for leaders. They identified seven connected processes formulated as dilemmas. A culture distinguishes itself from others by "preferring" one side of a dilemma's continuum. The seven universal dimensions of cultures are:

1. UNIVERSALISM versus PARTICULARISM

"What is more important, rules or relationships?"

The degree of importance a culture assigns to either the law or to personal relationships. In a universalistic culture, people share the belief that general rules, codes, values, and standards take precedence over the needs and claims of friends and other relationships. In a pluralistic culture, people see culture in terms of human friendship and intimate relationships.

2. INDIVIDUALISM versus COMMUNITARIANISM

"Do we function as a group or as individuals?"

The degree to which people see themselves function more as a community or more as individuals. In a principally individualistic culture, people place the individual before the community. This means that individual happiness, fulfilment, and welfare prevail and people take their own initiative and take care of themselves. In a principally communitarian culture, people place the community before the individual. Thus, it is the responsibility of the individual to act in ways that serve society.

3. SPECIFIC versus DIFFUSE

"How far do we get involved?"

The degree to which responsibility is specifically assigned or is diffusely accepted. In a specific culture, people first analyse the elements individually and then put them together—the whole is the sum of its parts. People's lives are divided accordingly and only a single component can be entered at a time. Interactions between people are very well defined. Specific individuals concentrate on hard facts, standards, and contracts. A diffusely oriented culture starts with the whole and sees individual elements from the perspective of the total. All elements are related and relationships between elements are more important than individual elements.

4. AFFECTIVITY versus NEUTRALITY

"Do we display our emotions?"

The degree to which individuals display their emotions. In an affective culture, people display their emotions and it is not deemed necessary to hide feelings. However, in a neutral culture, people are taught not to display their feelings overtly.

5. INNER-DIRECTED versus OUTER-DIRECTED

"Do we control our environment or work with it?"

The degree to which individuals believe the environment can be controlled versus believing that the environment controls them. In an inner-directed culture, people have a mechanistic view of nature; nature is complex but can be controlled with the right expertise. In an outer-directed culture, people have an organic view of nature. Mankind is viewed as one of nature's forces and should therefore live in harmony with the environment.

6. ACHIEVED STATUS versus ASCRIBED STATUS

"Do we have to prove ourselves to receive status or is it given to us?"

The degree to which individuals must prove themselves to receive status versus status simply given to them. In a culture with achieved status, people derive their status from what they have accomplished. Achieved status must be proven time and time again and status will be given accordingly. In a culture with ascribed status, people derive their status from birth, age, gender, or wealth. Status is not based on achievement but is accorded on the basis of the person's being.

7. SEQUENTIAL TIME versus SYNCHRONIC TIME

"Do we do things one at a time or several things at once?"

The degree to which individuals do things one at a time versus several things at once. Cultures developed their own response to time. Time orientation has two aspects: the relative importance cultures assign to the past, present, and future, and their approach to structuring time. In a sequential culture, people structure time sequentially and do things one at a time. In a synchronic time culture, people do several things at once, believing time is flexible and intangible.

So what does this mean for auditors when looking at culture across multinational organisations? Well, it impacts in two particular ways; firstly, has the organisation itself identified ways of working with its culture cross border, understanding and respecting individual cultures whilst remaining true to its own culture, behaviours, and values? And secondly, when undertaking fieldwork, workshops need to be refined and facilitated in a way that is cognisant of the country culture of the attendees. To miss this would be potentially to miss evidence in the fieldwork, or worse, to misinterpret it.

The approach that Alex had used in terms of storytelling by individuals was a positive one, especially as he had identified the need for everyone to tell two stories—one positive and one challenging or negative. This overcomes the challenge of individuals who only want to tell the positive or indeed the negative, and the challenges of groups where there can be dominant cultures, especially in groups from mixed locations. From an audit perspective, this gives more balanced evidence from large groups of individuals, which can be used to supplement document reviews and survey results.

Key Success Factors

- An application of emotional intelligence in understanding groups of individuals, whether that be within a country working with different culture or cross country

Design and Operating Effectiveness

As with any audit, design effectiveness and operational effectiveness are both key. We have seen many organisations that design the culture but fail to embed it. We have seen organisations where one part designs its own culture, often led by a charismatic leader, which causes confusion and challenges for both that team and others. And we have also seen organisations that don't even attempt to design culture, saying to us that "it is what it is," or "it's a result of our history," or "it's a function of who happens to work here."

Culture is a key enabler to the achievement of business goals and competitive advantage. You can copy a product and you can copy a system, but you cannot copy a culture.

So how do we go about design and operating effectiveness? As with other audits, we begin with a risk control matrix or risk control assessment structured by culture driver and assess the risks of each element with that driver for that particular organisation and its strategic goals.

Once we have that, we can produce a document request list, which for culture can be a little daunting as it covers all aspects of an organisation. Remember, however, that you are not auditing the governance or controls of the topic itself, you are looking at the effectiveness embedding of culture within the topic you are covering.

Despite the volume of documents, we are also able to utilise data analytics to assist. One effective example of this is to use analytics to analyse communications from various leaders and look for references to culture, behaviours, and values, both leader by leader but also over time. One aspect of culture change programmes we often see is a real focus on communication in the first year, with a gradual reduction as leaders assume everyone now "gets it." That can be interpreted by employees as leaders moving on to the next thing.

Desktop document analysis then needs to be supplemented with leadership interviews from the board down. We have included some of the questions you may want to ask in each of the chapters of this book; however, you also need to make sure that you cover the particular strategy of your organisation as well as your own measures of success.

With leaders, you are interviewing them from two perspectives. Firstly, you are trying to find out if they understand the "design" of the culture from the business strategy, and in particular the implementation of that design for any particular drivers they may be responsible for—so People Management for the CHRO and the balanced scorecard measures for the CFO. Secondly, you are trying to understand their personal buy-in as an organisational leader to the culture overall. How are they role modelling it? What is their level of personal buy-in? How are they communicating to their team? Is their communication and their personal tone from the top aligned and consistent?

Once we start to look at operational effectiveness, however, it can become challenging. You need to talk to both employees and leaders. With employees, interviews are not appropriate, especially at the very junior level. A focus group or workshop approach is much more suitable and enables employees to retain some anonymity and therefore contribute more openly. What does need to be managed, though, is the selection of the sample. You need a mix of tenure, a mix of experiences, a mix of genders, etc. The facilitation needs to be strong; in particular, watch for overly positive or overly negative people who may not only give unbalanced feedback themselves but can also overly influence the group.

In addition to this, each individual attendee is asked to provide two stories: one positive, when the culture was at its very best for them; and one negative or challenging, where they felt the culture let them down. This way, positive people need to highlight a challenge and vice versa, and we get balanced feedback from attendees. The contents of the stories themselves give an indication as to the scale or scoring of the topic raised. We have run workshops where employees were scratching around for *good* stories, and we have run workshops where employees were scratching around for *bad* stories.

Those leading the workshops need excellent facilitation skills—watching for silences, observing those who are quiet, and obtaining more information where the story merits it. This is exacerbated with cross-cultural workshops where particular care should be taken.

Once you have the workshop output and matched the stories to the culture drivers, then you can run the same workshop with leaders. Get their stories and look for both similarities and gaps. Feeding back the stories from employees is often a seminal moment in the audit—a real moment of realisation for leaders of the experience of employees telling them in stories what any number of survey scores could not. This approach to operational effectiveness can lead to an increased understanding of the risks and controls, and at this point can often lead to a need for further documents or follow-up interviews to ensure areas of higher risk are adequately covered.

What is also important to both design and operating effectiveness is measurement. For each element of each driver, does the organisation have a measure? And is that measure reviewed, considered, and potentially used to identify improvements needed?

Are the reviews regular and viewed as important by the leadership team? The importance of a set of clear KPIs is obvious, but they need to be balanced and there has been much discussion across many organisations as to the use of balanced scorecards. We are going further here and looking at whether the measures are not only balanced but also specifically aligned to and supportive of the organisation's specific culture that is aligned to its specific business goals. We want to see evidence of refinement and improvement based on measures, feedback, and outputs. We also want a structured prioritised view as to what will take the culture forward in the agreed direction and, most importantly, help the organisation achieve its strategic goals.

For all of this, the finance or strategy function can be critical. They will generally manage the balanced scorecard and its design, and the design should not be generic but should ensure that the balanced scorecard measures are linked to the specific long-term goals of the organisation.

Metrics to Look For

When auditing culture, most organisations already have metrics that can support the assessment of operational effectiveness. Whilst there is no single measure that provides a clear view—it is, after all, a complex and holistic subject—a basket of measures you can pull can provide supporting evidence.

Following are some examples:

- Employee survey, paying particular attention to any questions directly on culture and the embeddedness across the organisation. This is a good way to spot silos, especially as regards leadership or people management.
- Employee survey action plans and the completion ratio of those actions in the time stated
- Any organisational balanced scorecard information, looking in particular as to the balance the organisation places on financial, employee, and customer information and the alignment to the stated or designed culture
- Employee communication and the number of culture references, where you are looking for consistency over time and across senior leaders
- Employee turnover

- Employee exit interviews and any analysis of feedback

- Absence levels over time and by area. Particularly look for short-term absences and absences on Fridays and Mondays. Also look at the long-term absence as a result of stress.

- Learning days per employee per area and learning spend overall. Also look at the learning days per level of the organisation; it should not be absent at the top.

- Number of misconduct cases over time and the outcomes of those cases

- Number of whistleblowing calls, although these tend to be small in number and are frequently not enough for a sample

- Number of customer complaints, looking at type of complaints and time taken to respond. In terms of the type of complaints, any that are related to employee attitude or similar are worth exploring in more detail.

- Externally available culture information such as comments on sites carrying feedback from current and former employees

- Company scores and information available via Dow Jones sustainability index, FTSE4GOOD, or similar if the company participates in these

- Number and trend of employee grievances and any analysis of reasons, looking at trends over time and outcomes

- Participation rates in any company blogs, especially those of senior leaders where questions can be asked

- Metrics on processes critical to culture over time, looking at the impact of the process on customers

- Percentage of employees with objectives set within, say, one month of the performance year starting

- Percentage of annual performance review discussions held and forms completed—both elements of this are important

- Percentage of new starters undergoing induction training. We should have already looked at the induction training from a design perspective and ensured it included an introduction to culture.

- Any feedback on learning programmes, including consideration of a sample of free format feedback if included

- Percentage of time both the board and executive committee devote to culture. Clearly there is no right answer here; however, we would expect to see structured discussions, and not only at the stage that the culture is being designed. We would also expect them to be calling for metrics in this area and can utilise them in forming our opinion.

As organisations and audit firms progress in terms of data sophistication, the use of sentiment analysis on the conversations across the organisation via chat rooms, blogs, etc. can provide a more structured way of looking at this, which will be a welcome development. The more developed of the solutions in this space are aiming for enterprise-wide emotional intelligence enabled through data science. We are a little way off this at present, but we know that these areas are developing rapidly and it is worth bearing in mind when looking at possibilities, as some organisations will be moving in this direction.

Some organisations, especially in the financial services sector, are looking first to understand risk culture and here the metrics do overlap to a degree. However, the aim of a risk culture audit is to understand the embeddedness of risk awareness, assessment, and management across the organisation. When looking at the employee survey results, for example, the aim would be to focus in on an extract of different questions, those focussing on the understanding of and attitude to risk. The communications and conduct cases analysed would also be of those focussed on risk.

The challenge with both culture and risk culture metrics is that the auditor often has to source them from many different parts of the organisation—they are not always easily available. However, organisations that have a real focus on culture right from the top will often be able to produce them quickly. It is part of how the leadership manages and aligns the culture.

Joining the Dots

On Saturday, Alex decided not to think about his report for Monday. He had made lots of notes and everything he needed was within his grasp. However, he decided that he needed a day to rest. After all, he had been operating at full speed since the initial meeting. He had travelled up and down the UK, taken a trip overseas, and interviewed a lot of people. Today he needed some time to himself.

The latest Lee Child thriller was on his coffee table. Yes, he needed a different focus and, after making a coffee, he sat down and became absorbed in the exploits of Jack Reacher. The time ticked away and he was soon hooked on the story. In his mind, Alex saw himself doing a similar task to Jack. After all, Jack was an ex-military policeman who often had little to go on when attempting to solve a mystery. Jack would tug at all the threads, however small, and then gather them together to see what the bigger picture was. This was how Alex felt. He had started with little and now he had much information and needed to pull it together. He smiled at the parallel he had made and continued reading.

The following morning, Alex got to work on his presentation for the board. He had started to put notes into specific categories and now he needed to consolidate each of the categories. Then he needed to create a presentation with some strong visuals.

He divided his information into the drivers of culture—Strategy, Leadership, People Management, Resources, Processes, and Reputation. He then set about taking a story or two from each of the areas to enable him to offer real-life examples at the board meeting. Using some of the direct stories that employees had told him during his journey would make his presentation come to life.

Alex had been working for a couple of hours when he realised it was time for his Skype call with his mentor, Sarah.

"How is your cultural exploration going?" Sarah asked.

Alex bought her up to speed on all that he had seen and heard whilst on his journey. She was impressed with how much ground he had covered and asked how he felt about his upcoming presentation. Alex admitted he was a bit nervous but would do his very best.

"Imagine it's tomorrow and you are presenting. What will you be pointing out?" she asked.

Alex gulped and then outlined his findings across each of the drivers of culture. Sarah listened intently and he could see her making notes. As he spoke, he gained more confidence and it wasn't long before he was making some great points that she knew the directors would welcome.

Once he had finished, Sarah offered some further ideas and gave him feedback on what he had produced. It was a great conversation and Alex felt energised when he came off the call.

He needed to make a few changes, as Sarah had provided him with invaluable feedback. She had said, "Let's look at some key areas that you may want to develop further." Alex, as usual, decided to record their conversation. Following is an outline of his key points:

Strategy

The strategy of an organisation should include both the "what" and the "how." Strategy should include values, behaviours, and ethics. It should cover how the organisation is going to achieve its business goals and make it just as important a part of the overall strategy as what the organisation is aiming to achieve.

Leadership

Leaders must be able to reflect the strategy and articulate it, but also role model and live it out every day for their teams. They need to recognise it in others, bring their example to the fore, and reward it, either financially or through simple recognition or promotion. Every single day, every single conversation, and every presentation and action will be observed and noted. It can be challenging, but it can also be exhilarating when it works and takes on a life of its own.

Culture change will not be achieved overnight, but it is a myth to think that a change in culture can only be achieved over an extended period of time. A relentless focus on culture can see change achieved by large organisations with many thousands of employees over the medium term. Leaders need to design and implement measures so that the organisation knows they are paying attention to cultural issues and that the "how" matters.

People Management

Right across the employee lifecycle there are opportunities to nudge, shape, or reinforce the culture. From ensuring that new joiners are not only informed of the company's values, but that interviews, tests, and references seek out information about an individual's way of working, ensuring that individuals are recruited not just for their technical capabilities but for what they will bring to the culture and for their soft skills. This should then be reinforced through the performance management cycle, objective setting, talent identification, promotions, and every learning intervention.

There are many touch points where culture can be reinforced or enhanced. A company that puts real energy into this and makes every intervention count will find that the culture is not at all an accident of who happens to work there.

Resources

There are many messages given out that employees pick up on in terms of how organisations deal with their customers, supply chains, regulators, potential prospects, and with the way they manage the office space and the intranet and internet offerings. All of these messages need to be aligned and consistent. Otherwise, stakeholders such as employees and customers or clients will receive confused messages around the organisation's culture.

Process and Change

Some processes in particular are "critical to culture." For an insurance company, this could be the sign-on process or the claims process. For many companies, it can include the direct customer contact via the web or call centre. It is all the individual moments of truth where customers or employees touch the organisation, and the experience they have is really important.

It is also where the organisation is undergoing change, often with project management and new systems. Much attention is put into whether projects are on time and on budget, but very little is put on the impact of projects or transformation on the organisation's culture. Yet, these are critical times in terms of reinforcing culture and behaviour and the direction of both the "what" and the "how" of strategy.

Reputation

How an organisation portrays itself externally has a key part to play in the culture. Employees are a part of this audience. They see the impact and the position externally. They see positive and negative press, positive and negative impacts on the environment, and positive impacts on charities or local neighbours. It forms part of the holistic view of the organisation that they carry with them. It is vital that it is aligned and consistent and the impact on culture is positive.

Sarah and Alex talked for just over an hour. She had given away a lot of her intellectual property to Alex, but she didn't mind. She knew that helping Alex onward in his career was something to be proud of. She also knew that culture was her world and every day she learned something new that she could use. In fact, she was already making great progress on her next book and her upcoming lecture series.

Alex made some changes to his presentation and included some of Sarah's information. He had checked that she was happy for him to take it. Two hours later, he was all set. But his head hurt with the challenge of making a complex subject accessible to all. It was time for his run and it wasn't a moment too soon.

Reporting Back

Alex's slot to present at the board meeting was set at 10:15 a.m. He was pleased that it was early and he wouldn't have time to worry about it. Much better than having the slot just before lunch.

He felt in good spirits. His mentor, Sarah, had helped enormously. Knowing that he was free to use her material was such a gift, as was the story from every single employee from Shapers who had spent time giving their perspective and interpretation. To be fair, he had worked incredibly hard during the last two weeks to understand the subject of culture and then come up with a way of auditing it. Yes, he was pleased with what he had done. But, he just didn't know what level of understanding the board members had on the subject. Never mind. It's too late now, he thought.

At 10:10 a.m. he was ready outside the room where the board meeting was being held. Then at precisely 10:13 a.m. he was ushered in by the secretary who was taking notes of the meeting. Alex had a 30-minute slot to make his presentation and then take questions.

As he entered the room, he received a smile from Sam, the CEO, and that raised his spirits further. He nodded to the rest of the board and that was when he noticed Bill at the far end opposite him. Bill had an expression that said, "This had better be good." Alex gulped and then he began.

First came his opening: "The difference between a company that owns and manages culture and one where it is felt by the leaders to be impossible to manage is stark. Organisations that own and manage their culture actively are generally more vibrant, more engaged, more innovative, and more successful."

He continued. "So how on earth do you own and manage your culture? Well, a good leader would not let the strategy manage itself and it is equally true that good leaders do not let the culture manage itself. However, despite this, while many studies show there is a direct correlation between a healthy, productive culture and a company's bottom line, the majority of companies spend little time thinking, let alone doing, anything about this topic, even when they're spending lots of time thinking about their business strategy.

"So what is culture anyway? Well, some say 'it's how things are done around here' and we all intuitively know what that means, but we need to be more structured than that and really understand the drivers of culture. What we do know is that whilst the business strategy provides organisations with the 'what,' the culture provides them with the 'how,' and it is when a good strategy and a good culture work together that organisations really fly."

He paused and used his clicker to bring up the first of his slides to reinforce the key areas through visuals.

All the conversations, presentations, and documents that had helped him to understand the subject were distilled into one simple PowerPoint presentation. He understood the importance of keeping things brief and to the point. Plus, he only had 30 minutes anyway.

The first part of his PowerPoint showed the six key areas that he felt required auditing.

1. Strategy

2. People Management

3. Leadership

4. Resources

5. Reputation

6. Process and Change Management

He talked through each of the six areas and mixed in a short real-life example to further illustrate the point.

He continued. "The six drivers are not a pick and mix. You cannot decide to focus on three and believe that the others do not matter. They are the drivers because *all* of them matter, they work as a holistic system together, and any missing focus will mean that the overall culture will not be as effective as it could be at best, and that the drivers that are focussed on at great cost and effort will be wasted and misinterpreted at worst.

"So these are our six drivers of culture. The design, if you like. One that should be purposeful. Linked to strategic goals. And these formal drivers can be measured, can be audited, and can be reviewed in just as much of a structured way as financials."

The next section of his PowerPoint lit up with the heading Owning and Managing Culture.

Alex was now in his flow. There had been nods from around the board as he had highlighted issues that the company would need to look at. Bill was expressionless. Sam, on the other hand, was delighted as she kept nodding her encouragement.

He continued. "So how do you look at these culture drivers? Well, you need a structure for that too. This can be done through looking at each of the drivers with two lenses."

Design Effectiveness

"Firstly, we look for a defined approach for each driver and whether that approach is purposeful—managed and owned and linked back to the 'how' of the business strategy. Is it laid out consistently and does it have leadership buy-in? Here we are looking for rules, policies, and procedures that all align back to the business strategy, all playing a part in bringing the culture to life."

Operational Effectiveness

"Next we look at operational effectiveness and deployment. Is the approach evenly deployed across the organisation? Does it reach all areas? This is really important not just in terms of the inherent risk in a poor deployment, but because when it comes to culture, alignment and consistency are key. Any discrepancies in deployment will be noticed by employees who will draw the conclusion that 'you don't really mean it.' To understand operational effectiveness, we can examine evidence in the form of complaints, employee and customer surveys, and other feedback, but we also need to talk to employees at all levels. Engage with them and get them to talk to us about what works with our culture and what doesn't."

Measurement and Improvement

"What is also important to both design and operating effectiveness is measurement. For each element of each driver, does the organisation have a measure? If so, is that measure reviewed, considered, and potentially used to identify improvements needed? Is this review regular and viewed as important by the leadership team? The importance of a set of clear KPIs is obvious, but they need to be balanced and there has been much discussion across many organisations as to the use of balanced scorecards. We are going further here and looking at whether the measures are not only balanced but whether they are specifically aligned to and supportive of the organisation's specific culture that is aligned to the organisation's specific business goals. We also want to see evidence of refinement and improvement based on measures, feedback, outputs, a structured prioritised view as to what will take the culture forward in the agreed direction, and, most importantly, help the organisation achieve its strategic goals.

"I don't apologise for repeating this. It is worth reminding ourselves that this is the purpose of organisational culture. It can really enable the achievement of such goals, it is the 'how' of the strategy, and it is worth the ruthless focus, the passion, and the energy it demands from those responsible for its implementation."

Having gone through the six culture drivers and the two lenses, Sam waved at Alex.

"I think you have provided the board with a lot to consider. At this stage, any more in-depth detail and I think you would begin to lose some of us. What a great job you have done in just two weeks," she said.

Alex smiled. Bill grimaced and Sam spoke again.

"One final question before you leave. Can we now audit culture to CIIA standards with your framework and approach? If so, please proceed to draw up your team to implement this across the company as a whole."

Alex agreed that he would get started on the new project. However, just as he was due to leave, Bill spoke up.

"Does your culture work involve looking at potential mergers?" he asked. "Indeed it does," said Alex.

"In that case, can you be in a meeting in my office at 2:00 p.m. today? We are just starting to enter discussions with another company about working together. If a culture audit adds to our due diligence, then I welcome your work with open arms."

Sam nodded at Alex, who took the hint that it was his exit cue.

He left the board meeting already knowing he had just started his next journey of exploration. A merger of two companies, no less. What differences in culture would he discover?

Internal Audit Foundation
Sponsor Recognition

STRATEGIC PARTNERS

FOUNDATION PARTNERS

Larry Harrington
CIA, QIAL, CRMA

DIAMOND PARTNERS (US $25,000+)

GOLD PARTNERS (US $5,000–$14,999)

Natarajan Girija Shankar, CIA

Paul J. Sobel,
CIA, CRMA, QIAL

Pamela Short Jenkins, CIA, CRMA, *Fossil, Inc.*

Tow Toon Lim, CRMA, *DSO National Laboratories*

James A. Molzahn, CIA, CRMA, *Sedgwick, Inc.*

Frank M. O'Brien, CIA, QIAL, *Olin Corporation*

Sakiko Sakai, CIA, CCSA, CFSA, CRMA, *Infinity Consulting*

Anton Van Wyk, CIA, CRMA, QIAL, *PricewaterhouseCoopers LLP*

Yi Hsin Wang, CIA, CGAP, CRMA, *National Taipei University*

Ana Cristina Zambrano Preciado, CIA, CCSA, CRMA, *IIA–Colombia*

Internal Audit Foundation
Committee of Research and Education Advisors

CHAIRMAN
Tania Stegemann, CIA, CCSA, CRMA,
Catholic Professional Standards Limited (CPSL)

VICE CHAIRMAN
Angelina K. Y. Chin, CIA, CCSA, CRMA

STAFF LIAISON
Erika Beard,
Internal Audit Foundation

MEMBERS

James A. Alexander, CIA, *Unitus Community Credit Union*

Karen Begelfer, CIA, CRMA, *Sprint Corporation*

Subramanian Bhaskar, *IIA–India*

Despoina Chatzaga, CIA, CCSA, CFSA, *Exiger Limited*

Jiin-Feng Chen, PhD, CIA

Margaret Heim Christ, CIA, *University of Georgia*

Daniel Clayton, CIA, *University of Texas System*

Roslyn Y. Dahl, CIA, *Westfield Group*

Ozgur Baris Ekici, CIA, *Eaton Corporation*

Urban Eklund, CIA, CRMA, *Ericsson*

Carolyn Ferguson, *Trellis Company*

Nelson Gibbs, CIA, CRMA, *East West Bank*

Kivilcim Gunbatti, *Ziraat Bank*

Judy Gunther, CIA, CRMA

Yulia Gurman, CIA, *Packaging Corporation of America*

Beatrice Ki-Zerbo, CIA, *ifaci, Paris, France*

Mani Massoomi, CFSA, CRMA, *SoFi*

Joseph A. Mauriello, CIA, CFSA, CRMA, *University of Texas at Dallas*

Mark J. Pearson, CIA

Sundaresan Rajeswar, CIA, CCSA, CFSA, CGAP, CRMA, *Teyseer Group of Companies*

Bismark Rodriguez, CIA, CCSA, CFSA, CRMA, *Financial Services Risk Management*

Hesham K. Shawa, *IIA Jordon – International*

Deanna F. Sullivan, CIA, CRMA, *SullivanSolutions*

Jason Robert Thogmartin, CIA, CRMA, *Santander Holdings USA, Inc.*

Ashley R. Threeton, *ConocoPhillips*

Adriana Beatriz Toscano Rodriguez, CIA, CRMA, *UTE*

Jane Traub, CIA, CCSA, *The Nielsen Company*

Maritza Villanueva, CIA, *Regal Forest Holding*

Paul L. Walker, *St. John's University*

Larry G. Wallis, CIA, *VIA Metropolitan Transit*

Chance R. Watson, CIA, CRMA, *Texas Department of Family & Protective Services*

Klaas J. Westerling, CIA, *Intertrust Group Holding S.A.*